Build, draw & learn

with world-famous architects

This book has been done in collaboration
with photographer Jens Hemmel and
graphic designer Fie Sahl Kreutzfeldt.

www.hemmel.dk
www.fiesahl.dk

Malene Abildgaard
& Julie Dufour

Build, draw & learn

with world-famous architects

ABC
Forlag

Contents

Acknowledgements

We would like to thank the children and young people who "attend architecture" in their spare time at the Danish Architecture Centre, the Children's Culture House Ama'r and Farum Art School, who have all contributed to this book with drawings, models and invaluable feedback on the design exercises. A special thanks to Asa Cornish, Oskar Lauge Dahlberg, Miamaja Koch Olsson, Emily Patricio Ramos and Oskar Dufour Wiese.

The contributions of Jens Hemmel, our photographer, and Fie Sahl Kreutzfeldt, our graphic designer, have been indispensable, and we thank them for providing photos, ideas, layout, design and graphics.

Jane Lomholt has assisted with editing, translation and advice on the English edition of the book, and Henriette Bendix, Georgina Collins, Rebecca Lomholt as well as Birgitte Sandhagen have generously contributed with content, proofreading, translation etc.

We thank all of the above. And last, but not least, a huge "thank you" to our patient families!

Introduction

Welcome to a world full of building, drawing and learning in the company of architects known throughout the world.

In this book you will find inspiration for how you (and your family) can work with architecture. The book contains 10 different exercises, all of which are about the architect's methods and tools. Each exercise is connected to a relevant architect and a piece of architecture with the same theme or method.

In the exercises we have emphasized the breadth possible in architecture – taking it a step further than the superficial – to show some of the thoughts and methods behind working with architecture. In the beginning of the book you will find a list of tools and materials used by architects and at the end you will find a glossary.

This book invites you to work with the methods and tools, and at the same time it gives you interesting information regarding the selected architects and their architecture. When you read the book and work on the exercises, you will discover how many things you can change through architecture: light, atmosphere, function and much more.

Have fun building, drawing and learning together with world-famous architects.

Malene Abildgaard and Julie Dufour

Working as an architect

Architects add form to our surroundings, be they cities and buildings, landscapes or furniture. An architect is able to imagine something which does not yet exist, and an architect is able to pass his or her thoughts and ideas on to other people. This can be done, for instance, using drawings, photos or models.

To do this the architect uses a variety of tools. There is no simple answer to which is the most important tool, as there are so many ways of working with architecture. It all depends on how the architect prefers to work, which thoughts and ideas are going to be represented, and how they are going to be visualized. Is it a sketch by hand (page 66) or a sketch model (pages 144-145) that is showing the overall idea? Or a very precise drawing showing a lot of detail (page 97)? Or perhaps a presentation model of the final project (page 83)? Which tool you use depends on how you choose to present your ideas.

However, one tool is common in all of the architect's work, regardless of the type of project or way of working – and that is the use of scale. Scale is also known as measurement and size. The architect uses scale both in drawings and in model making.

In the following passage you can read more about scale.

Scale

The architect works with drawings and architecture models in different scales. The models, also called scale models, can present the entire project or a mere section of it.

Scale models are necessary for the architect to show his or her ideas before the project is built in real size.

Real size is a scale called 1:1 (pronounced "one to one"). A scale model can be either larger or smaller than real size. If the scale model is smaller than real size, for example 1:100, it means that the real project is 100 times larger than the model. If the scale model is larger than real size, for example 3:1, it means that the model is three times larger than the real project.

To remember which number comes before the colon and which number comes after the colon, you can use this conversion formula:

M:R

M = model
R = reality

This formula applies to both enlargement and reduction.

When you are working on an architectural drawing or model, remember to choose only one scale. Do not use different scales in the same drawing or model.

1:50   1:210   1:11   1:35   1:100   1:1

1:11,6   1:50   1:11   1:9   1:1   1:40

Build yourself in scale 1:50

Exercise

You can make your own scale figure, which will make it easier to work with scale in model making. Using the scale figure you can always check if, for example, the ceiling is the right height or if the windows are positioned so that you will be able to look out.

On the following pages you will find three different instructions on how to build your own 1:50 scale figure.

In two of the instructions you are building yourself in full figure. You can, of course, also make other kinds of scale figures – for instance, a person sitting down, a family, an animal, a car, a dog etc. And you can make scale figures in whatever scale you want, for instance 1:20 or 1:100. Use the conversion formula and instructions on page 17 to do this.

Materials

- Drawing paper
- Stiff paper
- Magazines

Tools

- Ruler or scale ruler
- Scissors
- Pencil or black felt-tip pen
- Glue stick
- Camera
- Possibly access to a printer
  and a photocopier

What to do

Method 1
Draw yourself

1. Draw yourself in full figure. At scale 1:50 you should be ca 3.5 centimetres high.

2. If this scale is too small to work with, you can draw in a larger scale and afterwards scale down your figure using a photocopier.

3. Cut the figure out and glue the figure onto a piece of stiff paper.

4. Build a foot to make your scale figure free standing.

Method 2
Take a photo of yourself

1. Take a photo of yourself standing in full figure. Print and scale your photo to 1:50.

2. At this scale you should be ca 3.5 centimetres high.

3. Cut yourself out and glue the picture onto a piece of stiff paper.

4. Build a foot to make your scale figure free standing.

Method 3
Find a person in a magazine

1. Find a picture in a magazine of a person standing. It is important that the person is the right height to create a scale figure in scale 1:50. At this scale your person should be ca 3.5 centimetres high.

2. Cut the person out and glue it onto a piece of stiff paper.

3. Build a foot to make your scale figure free standing.

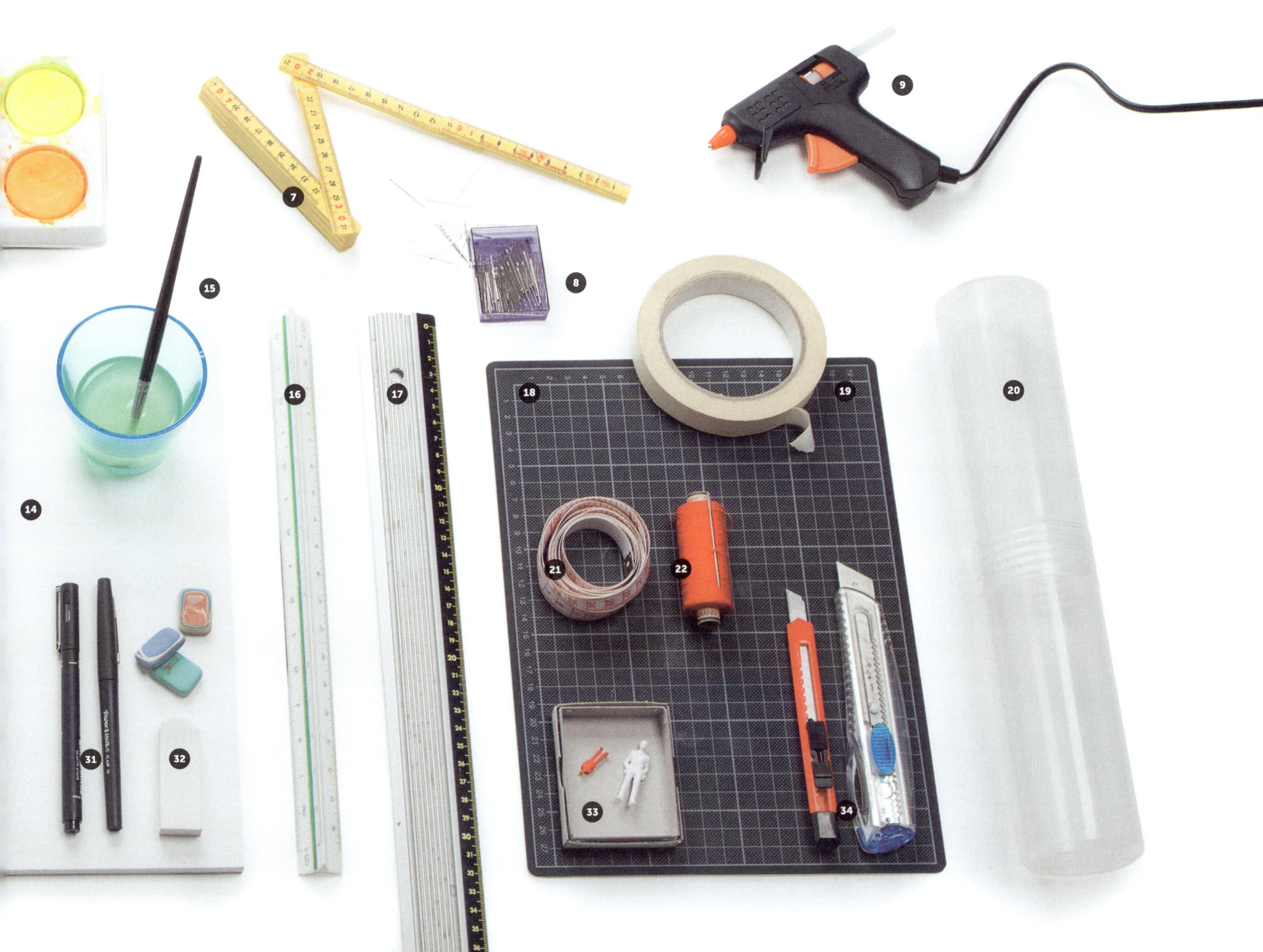

The architect's tools

1 Camera

You can use the camera on your mobile phone

2 Sketchbook

3 French curves

4 Chalks

5 Oil pastels

Useful for applying colour to photos

6 Neon watercolours

7 Measuring stick

8 Straight pins

9 Glue gun with glue stick

10 Dusting brush

Used to remove eraser dust from drawings

11 Tracing paper

*Thin, semi-transparent paper.
Used for tracing a drawing or parts of it*

12 Letter stamps and inkpad

Used for e.g. text on drawings

13 Watercolour travel kit

14 Watercolour paper

15 Water for water colouring

16 Scale ruler

*A ruler which shows six different scales,
for example 1:175, 1:100, 1:75, 1:50, 1:25,
1:20. Used for measured drawings involving
conversion of scale*

17 Metal straight edge

18 Cutting mat

19 **Masking tape**

20 **Drawing tube**

Used for storing and transporting rolled-up drawings

21 **Measuring tape**

22 **Needle and thread**

23 **Calliper**

Used for exact measurement of distance. Minimum distance: 0.1 millimetres. Particularly useful for measuring small, round objects

24 **Tweezers**

25 **Scissors**

26 **Glue stick**

27 **Squared paper/graph paper**

28 **Brushes**

29 **Pencils**

Graded from hard to soft

30 **Graphite or pencil leads**

Graded from hard to soft. Useful for shading in

31 **Felt-tip pens**

Available in different colours and widths

32 **Eraser**

33 **Scale figures**

(Read about scale in the chapter on Scale)

34 **Hobby knives**

The architect's materials

1. Grey card
2. Corrugated cardboard
3. Cork
4. Branch
5. Honeycomb cardboard
6. Stickers
7. Foam rubber
8. Styrofoam board
9. Corrugated plastic sheet
10. Semi-transparent plastic
11. Perforated cardboard
12. Tape
13. Tin foil
14. Moulded fruit trays
15. Polyester strapping
16. Rope
17. Cardboard *(from supermarket boxes)*
18. Stiff card
19. Quilted foil
20. Coloured paper
21. Squared paper
22. Marshmallows
23. Coloured transparencies
24. Champagne and wine bottle corks
25. Plastic strapping
26. Assorted wooden modelling sticks

27 Drinking straws
28 Four- or six-pack rings
29 Modelling grass, short
30 Non-slip matting *(fine mesh)*
31 Modelling grass, long
32 Corrugated card *(from cases of wine)*
33 Metal wire
34 Polystyrene packaging
35 Cord
36 Twine
37 Foam pipe insulation
38 Wire wool
39 Silver card

40 Plastic sacking
41 Non-slip plastic matting with pattern
42 Matchsticks, heads removed
43 Chicken wire
44 Plaster of Paris bandage

Nature as inspiration

Architects find inspiration in many different places. For the Danish architect Jørn Utzon nature was the greatest source of inspiration. From nature he got the idea to develop an additive building system, which can be expanded indefinitely. Let yourself be inspired by nature and try out the additive principle.

Nature as inspiration

Exercise

Inspiration can be found all around you; all you need to do is open your eyes and have an inquiring mind. Especially nature offers many peculiarities that can get your imagination going: crooked trees and branches, floating clouds, the whisper of the wind.

Carefully observe a small sample of nature at close hand. How is it structured? What is it made of? Build an architectural composition inspired by what you see. Your building material comes from nature: flowers with petals, leaves, stems etc.

 Materials

- Two-three flowers, for example
  dahlias, daisies, dandelions or similar
- Two sheets of styrofoam board
  or cardboard, ca size A3
- White drawing paper or watercolour paper

 Tools

- Scissors
- Tweezers
- Straight pins
- Pencil
- Thin, black felt-tip pen
- Colouring pencils or watercolour

What to do

Flower no. 1

1. Look closely at your chosen flower
   - What are the component parts
     of the flower?
   - Are they symmetrical?
   - What is the structure of the leaves?
   - Are there different colour nuances?

2. Separate the parts of the flower: stem, leaves, buds etc. Use a pair of scissors if necessary. Use a pair of tweezers if the elements are very small.

3. Place all the elements in order on a sheet of styrofoam board or cardboard and fasten them with straight pins. Place them in the correct order so that your display resembles a disjointed flower.

Tip

Look at a house in the same way as you looked at a flower: what are the component parts of a house?

Look at a town in the same way: what are the component parts of a town?

Flowers no. 2 and 3

1. Separate flower no. 2 in the same way as no. 1.

2. Place the elements on a sheet of styrofoam board or cardboard, but this time place the parts in a different order.

3. Imagine that each part of the flower is a space. For instance, each leaf can represent a room, the buds can be buildings, and the stem can be a path. Place the different elements so that they resemble a piece of architecture or a town seen from above.

4. Use flower no. 3 if you need additional parts for your composition.

5. Draw your composition so that it shows the kind of life you imagine is taking place in your building. You may wish to use watercolour paper for this. Colour your drawing.

Espansiva

A construction system inspired by nature

"Nature is my best friend and source of inspiration". These were the words of the Danish architect Jørn Utzon when he was once asked where he found his inspiration. For him, nature was a kind of laboratory where he could study at close range everything from plants to the sky and the sea. This gave him knowledge and inspiration, which he could use when he worked with his architectural designs.

The fact that Utzon was inspired by nature did not mean that he copied it. On the contrary, he observed how nature was constructed and what principles underlay the structure. For example, he would look at the structure of a tree. It was composed of three elements: a stem, branches and leaves. If you have those three elements you can construct a tree. What he found particularly interesting was that although all trees are composed of the same three parts there are no two identical trees. Why is that?

 Architect

Jørn Utzon
Denmark, 1918-2008

 Project

Espansiva
Denmark, 1969

Espansiva

The appearance of a tree depends on the conditions under which it has grown. How much sun, water and room there is, for example. You can say the same about architecture. The appearance of a house will also respond to the building site, the climate of the area and the needs of the people who live there. Because there is so much to take into consideration, it is often necessary to build a custom-made house; but that can be very, very expensive.

Utzon devised a construction system which consisted of modules. By combining a number of modules it is possible to build a house that responds to the building site, the climate and the inhabitants' needs. Utzon's modules were made of standard materials, that is, using standard dimensions and sizes. This is much cheaper than building custom-made houses.

Utzon called his system Espansiva and it was based on an additive principle. That means that you build by adding on, as in simple maths. The clever thing about the Espansiva additive system is that it is always possible to add another module. If you wish to expand your house, you just buy some more modules.

The system consisted of four different modules, which could be connected in innumerable ways. In principle the modules were identical, but they varied in size. In this way one module could serve as bathroom, one could serve as kitchen and one as bedroom and so on. Which module was used for what purpose depended on the desired size of that room.

Nature inspired Utzon to create the additive principle and Espansiva. The system represented new thinking in architecture – this possibility of endless expansion. Unfortunately, the system was never put into production. Only one Espansiva house was ever built, and it functioned as a show house. Today the house, located in Hellebæk north of Copenhagen, is in private ownership.

Two examples of the many ways in which Espansiva modules can be combined.

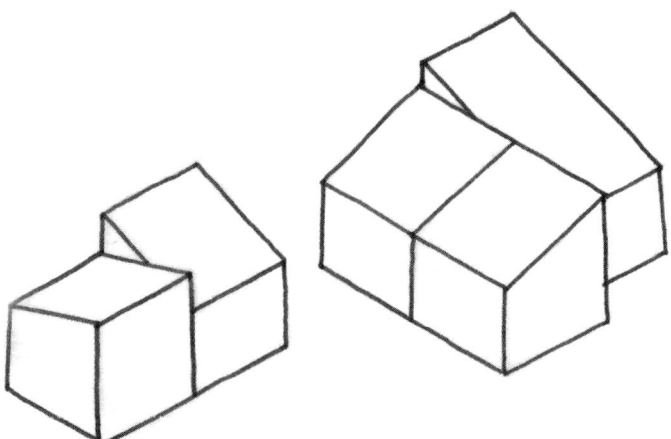

The Espansiva system consists of only four different modules, which can be combined in innumerable ways.

Nature is constructed according to a principle which Utzon called additive.
A single flower can grow into a flowering meadow by adding more flowers.
The same principle applies to trees and forests, houses and cities.
This was the inspiration for the development of Utzon's Espansiva system.

Nature as inspiration

The Sydney Opera House is Utzon's masterpiece and has made him famous around the world.

Nature as inspiration

Jørn Utzon

Most people know the Danish architect as the man behind the Sydney Opera House, the beautiful building with the big, white shells in Sydney Harbour. Utzon has never really explained where his inspiration for this building came from. Maybe it came from the sailboats, maybe from his travels around the world or maybe from nature.

Nature was part of Utzon's everyday life – both as a young sea scout when he got to know the sea and the sky, and as an adult when he always aimed to live near forests and the sea. Therefore, it was possible for him to get to know nature and to learn from it: the changing light, the scudding of the clouds, the movement of the waves and the colours of the sky.

In the world of architecture Utzon is often described as a genius. He had a very exact and precise way of working with materials and form, which he had learnt from his father, a boat builder. According to himself he was not good in school. He had difficulties with maths. However, he had a fantastic ability to work with geometry and to understand spatial relationships. This ability led to his education as an architect.

A career in architecture brought Utzon to many different places in the world, including the USA, Mexico, Morocco, Australia, Hawaii and Majorca. Some of these places he visited to seek inspiration; in others he settled down and worked. He often travelled with his wife Lis and their children, Jan, Lin and Kim.

Utzon received many prizes and awards during his career for his beautiful and original architecture. In 2003 he was awarded the prestigious Pritzker Architecture Prize.

Transform an everyday object

When creating architecture architects put emphasis on lots of different things, like shape, function, material etc. The Danish architect Bjarke Ingels emphasizes the element of surprise and the good story in his buildings. Create a piece of architecture with a fun story by transforming an everyday object.

Transform an everyday object

Exercise

Some buildings have the shape of everyday objects, and people often give these buildings pet names because of the likeness. For example, there is an office building in London called the "Cheesegrater"; an extension to the Stedelijk Museum in Amsterdam is called the "Bathtub"; and the Beijing National Stadium is often referred to as the "Bird's Nest". The pet names arise because of the shapes of the buildings, and the names become part of the buildings' narrative.

You too can create a building with a particular shape, setting the scene for a pet name and a story. To do this, pick an everyday object, such as a grater, and transform it into architecture. To get the best result and to have the most fun, choose an object with a space inside with which you can work. You can often find something in your kitchen or in a second-hand shop. Here you might be lucky and find an old baking tin, a toaster or a coffee maker which are ideal for a building project.

Materials

- Everyday objects such as kitchen utensils, machines, lamps and packing
- Cardboard
- Wooden sticks
- Transparent plastic
- Black drinking straws
- Small buttons and other plastic "odds and ends" for furniture model making

Tools

- Scissors
- Pencil
- Glue gun
- Hobby knife
- Metal straight edge
- Cutting mat
- Tools from the tool box – if you have to take something apart
- Possibly a scale figure in an appropriate size

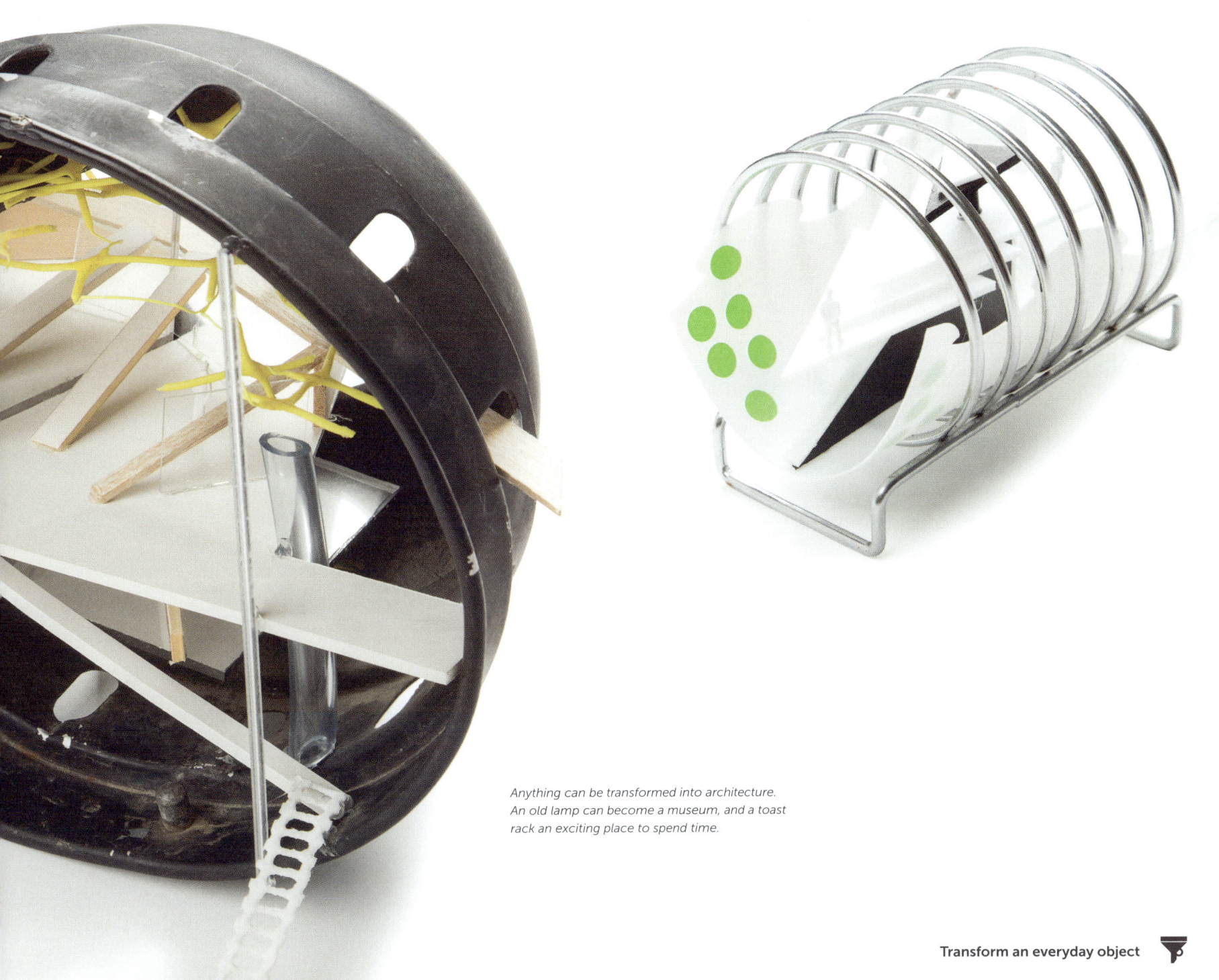

Anything can be transformed into architecture.
An old lamp can become a museum, and a toast
rack an exciting place to spend time.

What to do

1. Find a grater, a baking tin, a lamp or another everyday object.

2. Start by looking at your object. Does it have a space inside that you can work with? Does your object have to stand or lie down to create a space?

3. You can either choose to build inside or around your object. Or both.

4. Does the shape of your object give you an idea for a building design?

5. Make a decision regarding the scale of your building, e.g. 1:100 or 1:50. You can add a scale figure. (See the chapters *Scale* and *Build yourself in scale 1:50*).

6. Add floors, walls, columns, staircases, ramps etc. to your everyday object. See the *Tip* on page 59 regarding model materials.

7. What is the function of your building?

8. You can also give your building a title and pet name referring to the appearance of the building.

1

The Leadenhall Building in London has been named the "Cheesegrater". The building is created by Rogers Stirk Harbour + Partners.

2

The extension of the Stedelijk Museum in Amsterdam is referred to as the "Bathtub". The building is created by Benthem Crouwel.

3

The Beijing National Stadium is known as the "Bird's Nest". The building is created by Herzog & de Meuron and more.

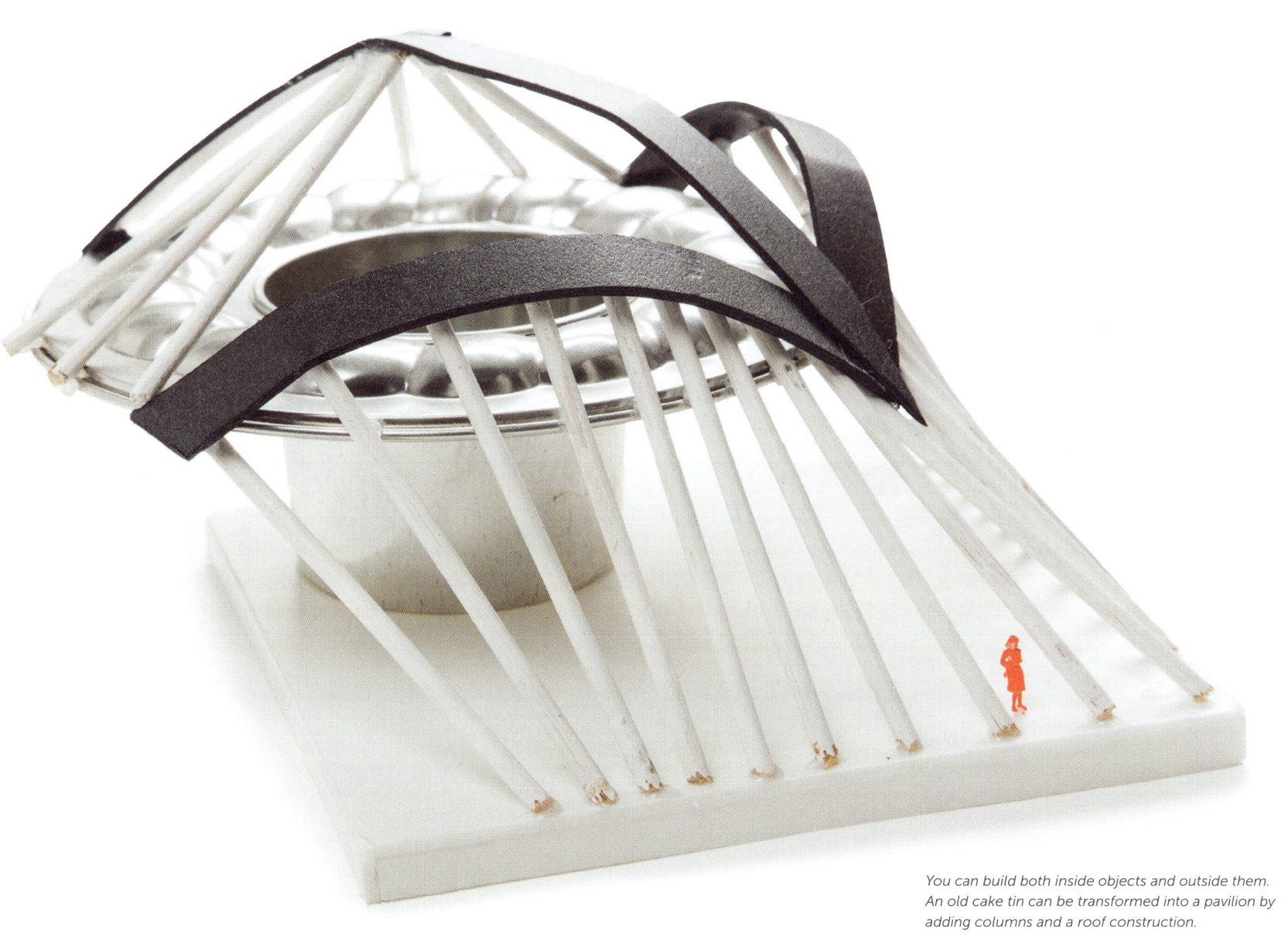

You can build both inside objects and outside them. An old cake tin can be transformed into a pavilion by adding columns and a roof construction.

Transform an everyday object

Tip

Some useful materials for model making:

Floors and walls
White or black styrofoam board

Columns
Black drinking straws or cardboard tubes

Stairs
Stiff paper or plastic strapping which can be folded into stairs

Ramps
Flat wooden sticks or stiff card

Windows or glass roof
Transparent plastic

Furniture
Small buttons, small screw caps or other small plastic thingamabobs for furniture model making

Amager Bakke will become the world's most sustainable power plant. The building will have a café, green areas and a ski slope on the roof.

Amager Bakke

A building with a story

The Danish architect Bjarke Ingels has designed the building Amager Bakke (Amager Hill). He has always been interested in architecture with a good story and his buildings are often given memorable names such as 8 House, the Mountain or Amager Bakke.

Amager Bakke is the name of a building in Copenhagen. It will be the world's most environmentally friendly energy plant. The plant will transform waste to electricity and heating. However, the most amazing thing about the building is that it will have a ski slope on the roof, 85 metres above ground level. Here you will be able to ski all year round. In addition to the skiing facility, there will also be green areas for running, climbing or walking.

From a distance, the people of Copenhagen will be able to witness the production of energy for the city, as the smoke machine inside the plant sends out smoke rings from a chimney – just like smoke rings from a pipe.

 Architect

Bjarke Ingels
Denmark, b. 1974

 Project

Amager Bakke
Copenhagen, Denmark (under construction 2014)

Transform an everyday object

A multi-waste-to-energy plant

An industrial building with rooftop recreational green areas has never been built before. Therefore, it is important to test the shape, function and materials of Amager Bakke before building it. One of the world's leading ski slope designers, International Alpine Design, has been working on the building's geometry. And the giant ski slope will have a special white plastic coating, enabling people to ski all year round – even on a hot summer's day.

Without doubt Amager Bakke will become a landmark in Copenhagen. The building is being constructed in an industrial area currently dominated by the present energy plant ARC. Situated on the waterfront and with various open-air recreational activities as neighbours, this area of the city will be transformed into an attractive destination for the people of Copenhagen and visitors alike.

It will be possible to go skiing all year round on the 85-metre high roof of Amager Bakke.

Amager Bakke is located by the water and surrounded by green recreation areas. It will be possible to pursue land or water sports here or just relax.

Bjarke Ingels

Bjarke Ingels' interest in architecture started when he was 10 years old. He loved building houses using LEGO®bricks – especially houses with secret spaces inspired by Batman and the villains in the James Bond films. These buildings have the most imaginative designs, incorporating secret doors, hidden rooms, movable bookshelves and underground swimming pools. Ingels has adopted the element of surprise and imagination in his architecture, continually producing wild and almost unthinkable projects. His architectural practice is named BIG (Bjarke Ingels Group), indicating big ideas and big projects. In addition addition to architectural projects Ingels is also involved with furniture design and industrial design.

An urban mini-space

Cities are full of spaces, just like buildings — but whether or not these spaces are pleasant to be in varies greatly. The Danish architect Jan Gehl is an expert on this matter. He is planning cities that create life between the buildings. Build a green urban mini-space which creates life and is pleasant to be in.

An urban mini-space

Exercise

When you walk or cycle through town, you will find that there are small, green spaces squeezed in between the buildings. Sometimes these spaces are used for growing flowers, maybe even vegetables and fruit. Occasionally there will be a bench where you can sit and rest, or you can exercise, or walk your dog.

Other urban spaces are filled with cars – no trees, flowers, benches or life.

You can create life between the houses in your town by building your own green space at small scale. First, find a place that could use a green makeover. By adding miniature furniture and potted herbs, for example, you can transform the place into a pleasant green urban space.

Materials

- A couple of small-scale pieces of furniture or other items
- A pot of chives, parsley or other green plants

Tools

- Sketchbook or pad of sketching paper
- Writing and drawing implements
- Camera
- Possibly a scale figure in an appropriate size

What to do

On-site survey

1. Pack a bag with materials and tools and go exploring in your area.

2. Find an urban space that could use a makeover. It could be a space between buildings or a square in the town.

3. Sit down and "feel" the place.
  - Where is it nice to be and why?
  - Who is using the space and what is the light like?
  - Is there a lot of traffic? Is it noisy?

4. Write and draw your findings in your sketchbook.

5. Also try to spend a whole day on your site and observe the changes in the light, shadows and movement of people. (See page 71 for an example of a photo survey).

Build a green space at small scale

1. Use your materials to create a pleasant green space.

2. Take a photo of your space at small scale and at worm's eye view. To do this you have to lie on your tummy with your camera.

Tip

Think about how much of your surroundings are included in your photo. For example, avoid a large bench or rubbish bin in your shot.

It is a good idea to have some buildings or trees in the distant background so that it feels like your space really exists in a context.

Photographic survey of an urban space on a summer's day.
Notice how the light and the atmosphere change throughout the day.

9:00 a.m.

12:00 noon

3:00 p.m.

6:00 p.m.

9:00 p.m.

Close-up of a green, urban mini-space.

Times Square after the transformation.
The place is still extremely active, but
now pedestrians and life between the
buildings have returned.

Times Square

A living urban space

One of the best-known urban spaces in the world is Times Square in Manhattan, New York. Times Square is known for its countless lit advertisements, confusion of traffic and crowds of people milling about at all hours.

The square was created more than 200 years ago when the city streets and avenues were first laid out. At the intersection of Broadway and Seventh Avenue a gap appeared which was then turned into an urban square. Over time the square became surrounded by buildings. One of these, built in 1904, is the headquarters of the New York Times, which gave the square its name. Throughout the 19th century the buildings became denser and taller, and the traffic increased immeasurably. This meant that it became more difficult to be a pedestrian there, and the life between the buildings disappeared. It was no longer possible to inhabit the space, to look around and to chat with others.

 Architect

Jan Gehl
Denmark, b. 1936

 Project

Times Square
New York, USA, 1904/2009

An urban mini-space

📷 An urban mini-space

Space to be

In 2007 the New York City Department of Transportation asked Jan Gehl to help with changing certain places in the city. The City Council wanted to make New York City, which was then dominated by vehicular traffic, more pedestrian and cycle friendly. One of their targets was Times Square.

One of the first things Gehl did was to examine how Times Square was used. He asked himself questions such as these: Who use the square? Where and how do people walk across it? How do they spend their time there? Answers to these questions were obtained by surveys – observing, counting, sketching, photographing and interviewing people. In this way he was able to form a picture of how Times Square was used.

The desired outcome was fewer cars and more pedestrians and cyclists. That meant that the possibilities for vehicular access had to be reduced and the possibilities for pedestrians and cyclists had to be increased. Gehl suggested that some traffic lanes be converted to bicycle lanes and pedestrian-only zones. In this way he closed off for large amounts of vehicular traffic and provided the possibility for pleasant spaces that could be occupied by people.

Times Square is still hemmed in by towering buildings, but it is far more hospitable than it was before. Now the square invites people to be users, as pedestrians, as occupiers, as cyclists.

The design of an urban space must invite pedestrians to spend time there.

Jan Gehl

The architect behind transforming Times Square is the Danish architect Jan Gehl. His architectural practis, Gehl Architects, is known throughout much of the world for its work with town planning, specifically taking into consideration the people who are to use, live and work in the areas.

When Gehl was a newly graduated architect in the 1960s, his primary interest was the aesthetics and form of his architecture. But then he met his wife-to-be Ingrid, a psychologist, and his focus shifted. She asked him why architects did not seem to be interested in people, a fitting question as architecture is made to be used by people. From that day on Gehl started to work with the life inside and between the buildings of a town. He started to examine how town planning can help change for the better, how we use towns and how we inhabit them.

In those years most towns were planned from a bird's eye perspective. The town was seen from above, ignoring how people felt as inhabitants of the town. That which we call human scale was not considered. But it exists in Gehl's planning. With his special ability to design a town so that it is pleasant to be in for pedestrians and cyclists, Gehl has created a whole new branch of town planning: spatial design.

Did you know

... that the human senses are developed so that we can experience our surroundings when we are walking? Therefore it is important that the design of an urban space invites pedestrians to be active, to stop up and to engage with other people around them. In this way we are able to create life in and between the buildings.

Zoo design

In Copenhagen Zoo there is a very unique elephant house created by the British architect Lord Norman Foster. It is a unique building because of its special considerations for the animals. But what needs do zoo animals actually have? And how do you design for them? Become a zoo architect for the day and design for a user with particular needs.

Zoo design

Exercise

How do you design for animals in a zoo? When you design for a special user the most important thing is to find out what needs this user has – in this case, a zoo animal.

There are many different periods of zoo architecture, each with its own view on animal welfare. Older zoo designs typically focused more on the visitor's ability to experience the animal than on the wellbeing of the animal. Often the animals were kept in cages, making it possible for children and adults to get close to the animals. In modern zoo designs there is much more emphasis on the animal's need for light, air and space – and this is reflected in the architecture.

You too can make a zoo design, taking into account the animal's special needs.

 Materials

- Cardboard – e.g. from a supermarket box
- Wine bottle corks
- Wooden sticks
- Black drinking straws
- Transparent plastic
- Tin foil

 Tools

- Toy zoo animals in an appropriate size
- Scissors
- Pencil
- Hobby knife
- Cutting mat
- Metal straight edge
- Glue gun

You can use all kinds of materials for your zoo project. It is a good idea to start with a base, maybe in heavy cardboard, which can hold your design. Remember, a rounded melon tray or similar makes a good cave or grotto.

What to do

1. You may already have a small plastic zoo animal. If so, you can use it as a scale figure in your model.

2. You can also make your own scale figure of an animal. See the instructions in the chapter *Build yourself in scale 1:50*.

3. Learn what needs your animal has. Does it need something to climb on? Or water for swimming? How does it get food? Does it need daylight? Consider whether your animal needs to be both indoors and outdoors.

4. Do not forget fencing. Should it be high, low, made of glass or perhaps a pool of water?

5. Besides looking at the animal's needs, also remember the zoo visitors. What is the best way for them to observe the animal? Are they going to stand on the ground and look in, or do they need to stand on something?

Tip

Some useful materials for model making:

Water
Mirror or tin foil

Concrete
Corrugated cardboard or other cardboard packing

Grass, bushes and treetops
Foam rubber, wire wool, knitting wool and artificial grass

Fencing
Wooden kebab sticks, black drinking straws, cardboard or transparent plastic

High-tech constructions
Old bicycle spare parts from your local bicycle shop

The Elephant House

A home with light and space

When we visit a zoo, we look at the animals. However, it is just as exciting to look at the architecture which secures the animals, making it possible for us to experience them up close, while protecting them. Copenhagen Zoo offers some interesting architecture – especially the new Elephant House.

The Elephant House is designed by the British architect Lord Norman Foster. It is a unique piece of architecture, which deals with the animals' specific needs. From the outside the building looks like two green hills surrounded by walls and columns. The hills have two large glass domes at the top.

The elephants also have a large outdoor zone with access to water – a pool where they can drink, bathe and play. Foster worked together with the Danish landscape architect Stig L. Andersson on creating the green facade and the outdoor zones of the building, making them blend in with the surroundings.

 Architect

Lord Norman Foster
Great Britain, b. 1935

 Project

The Elephant House in Copenhagen Zoo
Copenhagen, Denmark, 2008

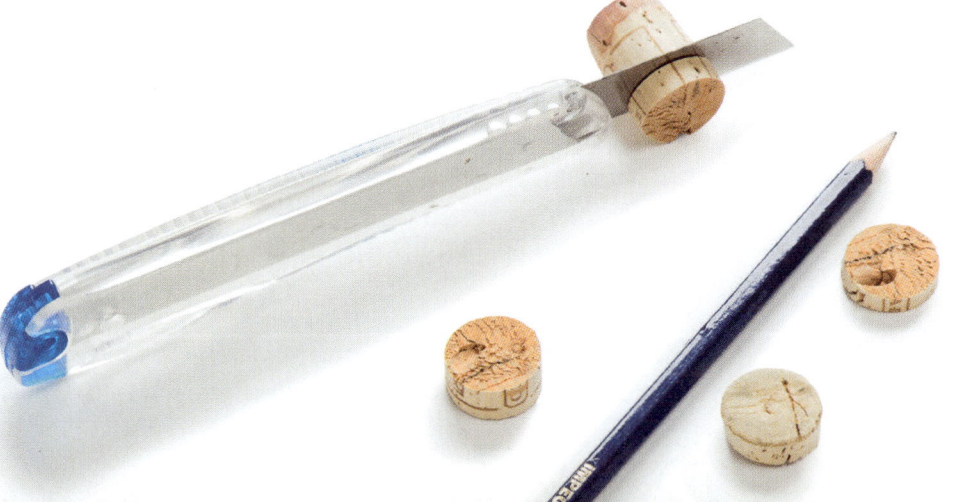

Zoo design

Light and elephant

Foster often includes skylight in his architecture and
the skylight is often shaped like a large glass dome. He
is a master of gigantic steel and glass constructions
that seem very light and elegant. One of his tricks is
the way he plays with light. The glass domes provide
the interior light, creating a pleasant atmosphere inside
the Elephant House. There is a "fritted" leaf pattern
on the glass domes, breaking and softening the light
– just like sunlight filtering through treetops in nature.

As a contrast to the light glass construction, the
walls and columns of the Elephant House are cast in
concrete. Inside the house rows of concrete columns
and ropes separate the elephants and the visitors. In
the outdoor zone concrete columns are a positive
challenge to the animals when looking for food.
The zoo keepers hide the elephants' food behind
the columns, and the animals then have to use their
trunks to get to the food.

Lord Norman Foster

Foster always works with the latest building technology. That is why his designs are called high-tech architecture. He is world-renowned for his functional and simple buildings in steel and glass. He finds inspiration for his buildings in for example aircraft design. As a matter of fact he loves aircrafts and he loves flying.

As a young man Foster did his military service in the British Royal Air Force, where he experienced aircraft design at close hand. When you design an aircraft you have to use the latest technology; you also have to find the optimal form for the desired function. This inspires Foster.

Today, he is a world-famous architect, designing and building architecture all over the globe. He has received many prestigious architectural prizes, such as the RIBA Gold Medal and the Pritzker Architecture Prize. In 1999 he was created a life peer as Baron Foster of Thames Bank and is now formally addressed as Lord Foster.

Does your room work?

A house should be just as efficient as a machine. And it should be done up in a functional way without useless bric-a-brac. This is what the Swiss-French architect Le Corbusier believed in as he wanted to improve people's lives through architecture. Test your room — how well does it function? And why not make a new proposal — if you need to.

Villa Savoye

Does your room work?

Exercise

How well do you know your room? Does your room work for you? For a room to really be functional, it is important that you give some thought to where you position the furniture in relation to how it is used. Have you thought about whether your bed is in the right place, or if there is enough light at your desk?

Survey your room and make a sketch of its floor plan. Evaluate how functional it really is.

Draw a proposal for rearranging your room so that it works better for you.

Materials

- Squared paper
- Coloured paper

Tools

- Measuring stick or measuring tape
- Pencil
- Scissors
- Fine, black felt-tip pen
- Ruler
- Glue stick

Quick sketch of a room seen from above.

Scale drawing of a room, scale 1:20.

Scale drawing of a room with changed interior, scale 1:20.

What to do

Surveying

1. First do a rough sketch of your room on squared paper.

2. Measure the length and breadth of your room and add the measurements to your drawing.

3. Mark the location of windows and doors and note down their measurements.

4. Measure the length and breadth of your furniture and add them to your sketch. Note down the measurements on the drawing.

5. You now have a sketch drawing of the floor plan of your room.

Make a scale drawing at 1:20

1. Recalculate all the measurements on your drawing so they correspond to scale 1:20. Read about scale in the chapter on *Scale*.

2. Use the new measurements, scale 1:20, to make a new drawing of your room (without the furniture and measurements). As this should be a precision drawing, you should use a ruler and a fine, black felt-tip pen.

3. Colour in, hatch or otherwise fill out the thickness of the walls. This makes it easier for you to see where the door and windows are.

4. Now you have a scale drawing of the floor plan of your room at 1:20.

Is your room functional?

1. Draw your furniture on a coloured sheet of paper at the same scale as your room (1:20). Cut out the pieces and place them on your plan.

2. Have a good look at your plan:
   – Could the furniture in your room be arranged in a better way?
   – Is your bed in the right place with regard to light and noise?
   – Is your desk placed so that it gets lots of daylight?
   – How do you store clothes, shoes, books and so on?

3. Try to place the furniture differently on the scale drawing.

4. When you have found a good solution, glue the furniture down.

Villa Savoye

A machine for living

The Swiss-French architect Le Corbusier once said that "The house is a machine for living". By this he meant that a house should be as practical and efficient as a machine.

A house has to fulfil certain needs; for example, it has to provide a place for eating and a place for sleeping, but apart from that nothing else is strictly necessary. The architect would say that a house has to be functional. Le Corbusier built several different kinds of functional "machines for living". One of them is the Villa Savoye near Paris in France.

 Architect

Le Corbusier
Switzerland/France, 1887-1965

 Project

Villa Savoye
Poissy, France, 1931

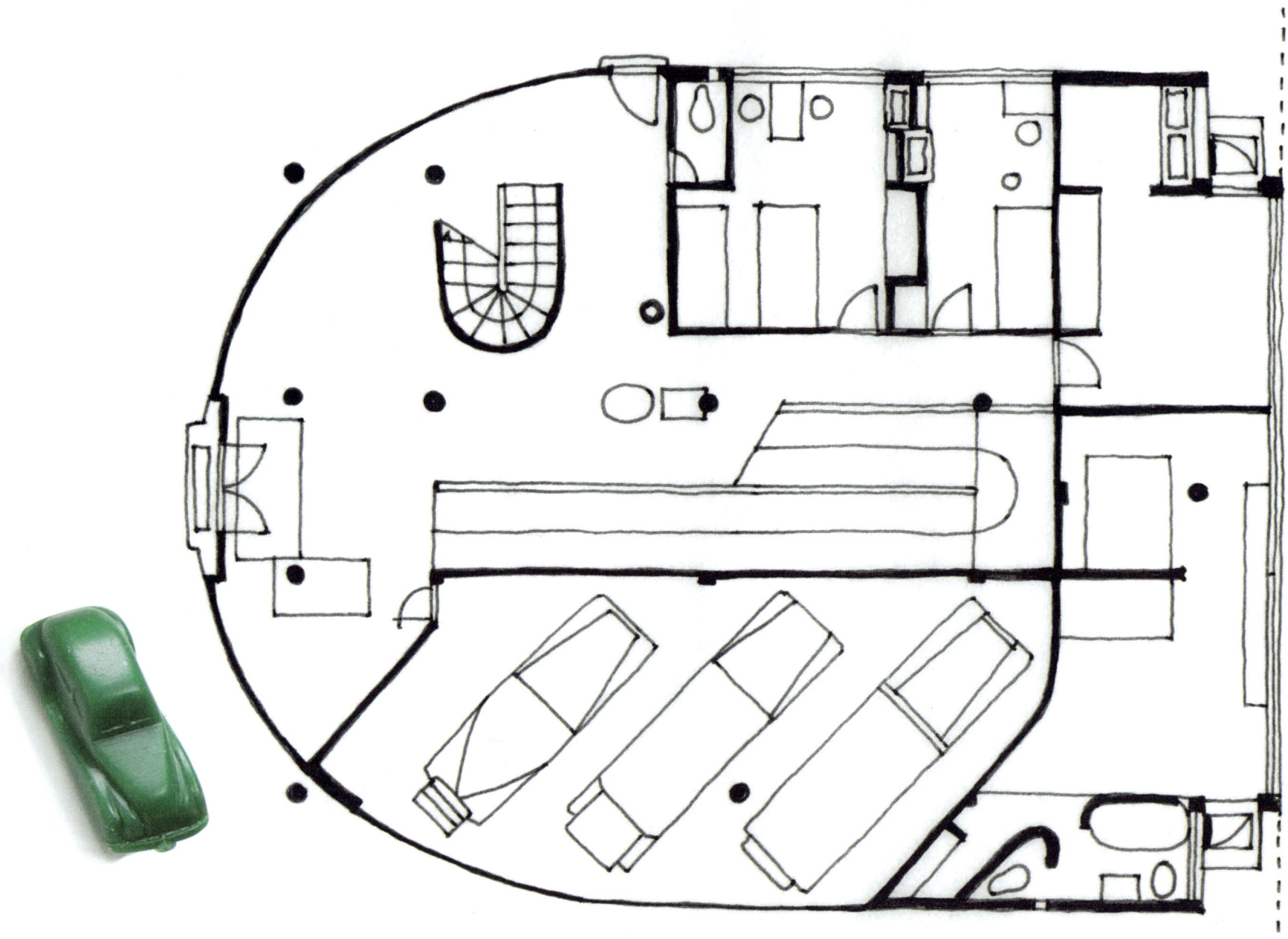

Zoo design?

Form and function

The Villa Savoye was built at a time when people were exploring new ways of living. In architecture this period is called "Functionalism" (also referred to as Modernism). During this period it was felt that everything in a building had to serve a purpose. If it did not, it was superfluous. Buildings, inside and out, were stripped of all decorations and bric-a-brac.

Many architects, including Le Corbusier, followed the motto "form follows function". Basically this means that the various functions of a building influence the form and appearance of the building. Le Corbusier was inspired by the designs of cars, airplanes and ocean

Ground level floor plan of the Villa Savoye. Notice how the drawing gives information about the period when the house was built, the house itself and its inhabitants. For example, there is room for three cars in the garage, and only one of the rooms has a private bathroom – the other two would have had to share. These rooms were for the servants.

Inside the Villa Savoye there are plenty of daylight and good vistas.

liners, because all these are designed according to their function, both in relation to their external form and their internal layout.

The Villa Savoye was designed to be functional. The house had to provide shelter from the heat, the cold and the rain. It also had to contain a certain number of rooms for specific functions: a room for cooking, a room for eating, a room for relaxing and so on. One room for each function. The general idea was to think about the functions needed in the house from the very beginning of the design process, so that each function was allocated its own place. For example, the Savoye family was one of the first families in their area to have a car. So of course, a place for the car had to be considered in the general design. This is why a part of the ground floor functions as a garage.

Other important elements that were considered from the very beginning include daylight and the view. The idea behind this was the conviction that both were important for a healthy life.

Le Corbusier therefore designed horizontal ribbon windows on all four sides. These four elevations and the fact that the building is white on the outside and almost throughout the inside give it a spacious and airy feeling with open views onto the green outdoors.

Today the Villa Savoye is a national monument and is open to the public all year round.

Le Corbusier

Le Corbusier can usually be recognised by his bow tie and heavy, black-rimmed, round glasses. He is often referred to as an architect, but he worked in many different creative fields. Apart from designing houses, cities and furniture, he was also a writer, a polemicist and an artist working with paints, etchings and sculpture.

As a young boy Le Corbusier studied the landscape around his home. He always had a sketchbook in his pocket and enjoyed drawing and painting what he saw. This means that there are more than 100,000 drawings and paintings by him today.

He received his first architectural commission when he was 18 years old. From them on his career took off, and today Le Corbusier is considered one of the most important architects of the 20th century. This is mostly due to his belief that architecture can improve people's lives.

Cave design

When architects need to test an idea, they can use scale models, but they can also ask the future user: "what do you think?" This is precisely what the Danish architect Dorte Mandrup has done regarding a completely new Children's Culture House Ama'r. The result: a building containing a lot of caves. Build your own cave model 1:1 where you decide on the shape and content.

Cave design

Exercise

Sometimes architects need to test an idea in actual size (see the chapter on *Scale*). A model in real size can be anything from a detail on a facade to a small room. The model can be made of typical modelling materials like cardboard or wood, or it can be made of the materials chosen for the final design.

Using a 1:1 model makes it possible to test, for example, if a cabin has the right dimensions for a good night's sleep, or if a chair is comfortable, before it goes into production.

You too can try to build a model in 1:1 by constructing a cave.

Materials

- Two-three bed sheets
- Possibly a piece of cotton jersey e.g. an old T-shirt

Tools

- Pencil
- Drawing paper
- Rope
- Safety pins
- Clothes pegs
- Torch, pillows, blankets etc.
- Possibly small clamps, a measuring tape, scissors, needle and thread

What to do

The architectural design of your cave will depend on three things: the place where you choose to build it, the materials you use to build it with, and the purpose it will have.

The location for your cave can be indoors or outdoors, like in a garden or the woods. Your materials can include everything from branches and boards to cloth and tarpaulins. Your cave can serve as a place to hide or to relax, or maybe it can be a lookout post, or something completely different.

In this exercise you are building an indoor cave made of fabric. The openings into your cave should be flexible so that it becomes a kind of multi-purpose space where it is possible for you to both hide and invite others to come in.

1. First you have to find a suitable indoor space for your cave. It is a good idea to make a plan drawing (see an example on page 97) of the space before you start to build. This way you can more easily decide where to fix the rope that will be the loadbearing structure of your cave.

2. Now you need to prepare the bed sheets you are using for the cave. Since the cave has to have flexible openings, you should be able to lift the edges of the fabric to form openings and fix the openings in an "open" position. You can use safety pins or clothes pegs for this, or you can use strips of the jersey material to make ties. The advantage of using jersey is that it does not fray.

3. Lay out your rope in the same way as in your drawing and fix it to at least three points. If there is nothing to tie the rope to, use clamps instead.

4. Hang your sheets over the ropes. The sheets should extend all the way to the floor so that they become the walls of the cave. Use ties, safety pins or clothes pegs to keep the sheets in place.

Tip

You can experiment with the points you use to fix the rope and notice how the cave changes form depending on the slant and height of the rope.

You can also try to use other materials for the walls of the cave and see what effect this has on the shape of the cave and on the light inside.

Did you know

… that there are many different kinds of caves? There are natural caves, like dripstone caves; caves constructed by animals or people to protect them from the weather; mobile caves like tents; and magical caves like Aladdin's cave in the fairy tale "One Thousand and One Nights".

There are different kinds of caves throughout the
Children's Culture House Ama'r. The "Love Cave"
is lined with red felt, full of big cushions and has a
window into the "Hall of Possibilities".

The Children's Culture House Ama'r

A house full of caves

The Children's Culture House in the Amager district of Copenhagen is the world's first purpose-built house of culture for children – and by children. What is so special about the house is that children have taken part in designing it. Perhaps that is why there are a lot of caves in the building.

At the Children's Culture House Ama'r children from 0-18 years of age attend lessons in their spare time in art, architecture, dance, drama, music, role play and much more. They can take part in open weekend workshops together with their families, or they can visit the culture house on weekdays together with their class or after-school club. Together with the

Architect

Dorte Mandrup
Denmark, b. 1961

Project

Children's Culture House Ama'r
Copenhagen, Denmark, 2013

The first things you notice about the Children's Culture House Ama'r are the slanting roof, the big wooden-framed windows and the aluminium sheeting on the roof and walls.

professional artists, architects, dancers and musicians in the house the children take part in the planning of activities.

The Children's Culture House Ama'r is designed by the Danish architect Dorte Mandrup. As part of the design process, groups of children provided architectural ideas for the content of the culture house. The children worked on how the floors, walls and furniture could be designed. As a result, a set of principles were produced and incorporated into the design.

As you enter the culture house, it is obvious that children have taken part in designing the architecture. For example, the children wanted to be able to spend time alone together with a good friend in smaller spaces. This wish has been fulfilled with the many caves and the large bay windows, perfect for seating and playing. The element of surprise was another wish, implemented in a ceiling resembling a meadow with flowers, and a toilet where you can draw with chalk on the black walls while listening to stories.

It is possible to play and move about throughout the Children's Culture House Ama'r; there is even a climbing wall.

Fun architecture

The Children's Culture House Ama'r is located in a densely built and charming part of Copenhagen. Here you find a mix of housing, shops and cultural institutions focusing on music and children's theatre. The house is tucked away next to a kindergarten and some housing.

The architecture is like a folded piece of paper with sharp edges and surfaces set at specific angles. When the culture house went up, the next-door neighbours were nervous about the building overshadowing their courtyard garden. However, the roof surface dips and the walls are set at an angle that actually lets sunlight into the courtyard.

Already when you enter the culture house, you sense that there are many surprising and fun spaces hidden away and spread out on several levels. There are staircases leading in different directions; there is a large climbing wall, an open workspace and a "Hall of Possibilities". And there are caves with different themes, such as the LEGO® cave covered with LEGO® bricks and building plates, and a "Love Cave" lined with red felt and soft cushions.

Cave design

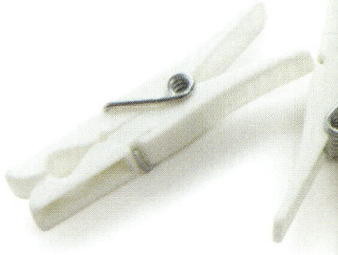

Dorte Mandrup

The Danish architect Dorte Mandrup is known for her aesthetics, running through her designs to the smallest detail. Her architecture stems from the Scandinavian design tradition, which includes beautiful and simple solutions and high-quality materials.

Mandrup emphasizes the user and the functionality of a building. That is why she involves the future users in her design process. It is also important to her that a building fits into its surroundings. She finds the architecture of a building uninteresting if it is just a piece of sculpture. Good architecture is creating the possibility for enjoyment and a good life. The Children's Culture House Ama'r is a fine example of this with its large open multi-functional spaces and small caves tucked away throughout the house.

Mandrup has designed many different kinds of buildings, from a summer cottage to a transformed water tower, and now also the world's first new-build culture house for and by children.

Architectural collage

The architecture by the Spanish architect Antoni Gaudí is best characterized as fantasy. His buildings are like colourful collages full of elements from nature and fairy tales. Free your imagination and build your own architectural collage full of fantasy.

Architectural collage

Exercise

You can create an architectural collage by building layer upon layer of all sorts of images from newspapers, journals, magazines, advertisements etc. Anything that is flat can be used, including bits of wallpaper, gift wrapping paper and sweets wrappers.

Using the shapes, colours and structures you have chosen, you can build a room and create a fantasy universe.

There are different ways to make a collage. Maybe you decide to cut out and use only green images. Or maybe you want to use special figures and objects, which can create focus in your space.

Have a go at creating a house or a room inspired by nature or a fairy tale. Use your imagination. In the world of collages anything is possible.

Materials

- White paper
- Newspapers
- Magazines
- Photos
- Coloured paper
- Tape
- Stickers

Tools

- Scissors
- Pencil
- Glue stick

What to do

1. Start by drawing a rough sketch of a room or house on a sheet of white paper. Then cut out all different kinds of motifs from magazines, newspapers etc. They can be funny, ugly, beautiful, crooked or coloured – you decide. You can also try gently tearing them out – that gives a nice, uneven edge.

2. While you are looking for your motifs, try to imagine what you want to communicate with your architectural collage. When you combine different motifs, they sometimes acquire a new meaning. For example, if you cut out the eyes of a portrait and place them on a motif of a piece of furniture, the furniture will almost appear to be alive.

3. Place your motifs on your drawing – loosely, without glue. This way you can move them around in relation to each other; or you can cut into them, changing their shapes. When you are satisfied with your collage, glue the pieces down.

4. Consider which colours you want to use. For example, if you have a lot of green, using a red motif as contrast might be a good idea.

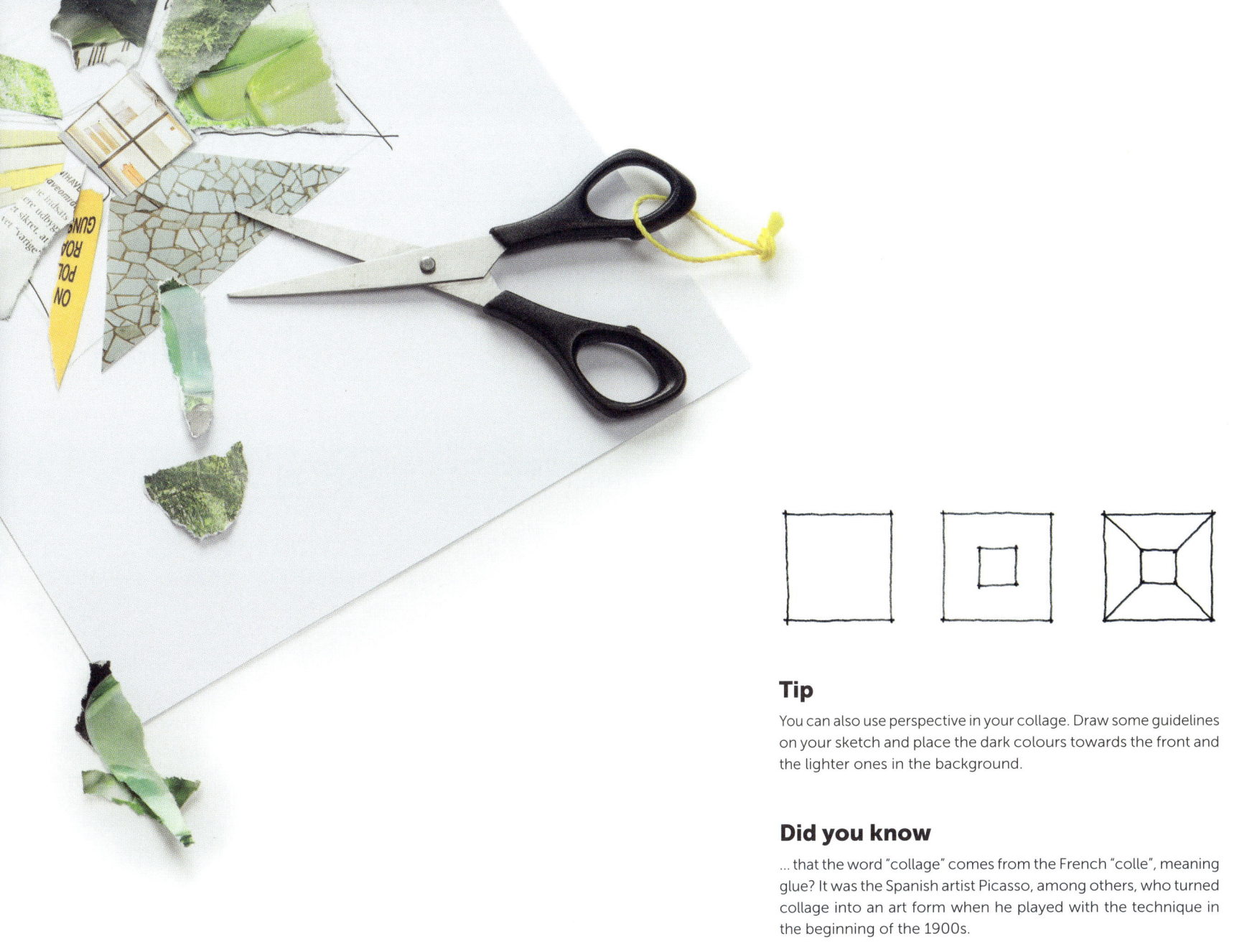

Tip

You can also use perspective in your collage. Draw some guidelines on your sketch and place the dark colours towards the front and the lighter ones in the background.

Did you know

... that the word "collage" comes from the French "colle", meaning glue? It was the Spanish artist Picasso, among others, who turned collage into an art form when he played with the technique in the beginning of the 1900s.

Casa Batlló

A collage of colours and forms

Casa Batlló (the Batlló House) is located on one of the main streets of the Spanish city, Barcelona. The house is very different from the other houses in the street. It looks as if it has just stepped out of a fairy tale.

It has been said that the house is inspired by the legend of St George who killed a dragon and saved the life of a princess. If you look closely at the roof ridge, you can see the dragon's back and the hilt of the sword St George plunged into him. The surrounding balconies resemble bird skulls, maybe from birds eaten by the dragon? Another interpretation is that the hilt of the sword is not a sword at all but the tower where the princess was kept prisoner. If there is a dragon, there has to be a princess to be rescued. Or not ...?

Architect

Antoni Gaudi
Spain, 1852-1926

Project

Casa Batlló
Barcelona, Spain, 1904

A fantasy house

Antoni Gaudí was commissioned by the wealthy industrialist Josep Batlló i Casanovas to rebuild an existing townhouse. Gaudí was given carte blanche. He peeled off the existing facade, constructed additional floors and created quirky solutions and details.

Gaudí, who was inspired by nature, believed that all that an architect needs can be found in nature in its natural form. The new facade had numerous columns that resembled bones or parts of plants, and it was clad in a glass mosaic skin. Initially, Mr Batlló was anything but pleased with his new house. It looked like nothing he or others had ever seen before, and his neighbours made fun of it. It received several pet names, one of which was La Casa dels Ossos, the "House of Bones". But before long, people realised that it was a very special piece of architecture. Today Casa Batlló is a listed building visited by thousands of guests annually.

Casa Batlló is from a time when new architectural styles were emerging. This style is called Art Nouveau, meaning New Art. This new style was applied to everything from furniture design to fashion design and jewellery. The inspiration was nature's own soft lines, which you can see in insects and plants.

Although Casa Batlló has several characteristics of Art Nouveau, it is completely in its own category, both inside and out. The inside gives the impression of the belly of an animal. All the same, most people have said that they feel at home in the fantasy rooms of the house – even on the roof, which is accessible, where you can see the dragon at close range and a band of horsemen, which the chimneys suggest.

In addition to nature, fables and legends greatly inspired Gaudí.
At Parc Güell the dragon here guards the underground water storage.

Did you know

... that Gaudí often worked closely together with the builders and craftsmen? He once got a builder to sit in a plaster mould of a long snake-shaped bench for Park Güell to ensure that the bench would be comfortable to sit on.

Antoni Gaudí

Antoni Gaudí is a famous Spanish architect. Already as a child Gaudí was interested in nature and its forms. He spent much time studying nature because he was unable to run around and play with the other children; he had arthritis.

Gaudí was not particularly good at school, but he showed interest in the universe of geometry. As he was good at being creative and at drawing, he applied to the school of architecture in Barcelona. Many people did not understand his architecture. Not until the wealthy Eusebi Güell began supporting him financially and became his patron did Gaudí become a popular and renowned architect.

During his long career as an architect Gaudí designed many houses for wealthy families. He also designed a park, Park Güell, situated up above the city of Barcelona. Common to all his work is a strong element of fantasy. His masterpiece is the cathedral La Sagrada Família (the Church of the Holy Family), which he worked on for over 40 years without completing it. Gaudí was 31 when he started to design the cathedral, but 25 years passed before the first bell tower was up.

Towards the end of his life Gaudí worked on the cathedral day and night; he even had his bed moved onto the building site. Sadly, Gaudí was killed, run over by a streetcar. After his death his drawings for the cathedral disappeared, and the architects who took over his work have often had to guess at his intentions.

Building work is still going on at La Sagrada Família. When you visit it, you can see Gaudí's grave in the crypt underneath the cathedral.

Soft pavilion

Can a building flow? The Serpentine Sackler Gallery pavilion can
— almost. The Iraqi-British architect Zaha Hadid has designed the
pavilion. She is known for working with soft, organic shapes and she
often experiments with new technology and materials. You too can
experiment with soft shapes and materials when you build your own
pavilion — in tape.

Soft pavilion

Exercise

Perhaps you have come across a pavilion in a park or been to a party in a garden pavilion? Pavilions are made of many different materials and they come in various shapes and sizes. They can also have many different functions. Some pavilions are just temporary, like a party tent in a garden. Others have a more permanent use, like a tea pavilion or a small gallery in a park. Some pavilions are made of wood and some are basically steel or iron constructions. And others have a soft material like canvas as the main material.

Thanks to technology we are now able to create a lot of different soft and organic shapes. Why not try creating one yourself?

Materials

- A building base of black cardboard or plastic e.g. size A5
- Tape

Tools

- Sketchbook
- Drawing implements
- Scissors
- Scale figure in an appropriate size
- Possibly a camera

What to do

1. Go for a walk in your local park and imagine that you are designing a pavilion for the park.

2. Find a suitable location and draw the location in your sketchbook. You can also take a photo of the location. Remember that your pavilion can be freestanding or connected to an existing building.

3. At home, sit down at your desk with your building base and start model making. The tape is your building material.

4. Explore the material – it has a lot of possibilities. You can quickly construct a small space by creating a loop using just a strip of tape. Remember that the two ends should overlap so that the sticky side is on the outside. You can continue making loops resulting in a facade with openings or rooms.

5. Think about the function of your pavilion and where the entrance is. You can build a portal or an entrance by fastening a piece of tape in two places on your building base.

The simplest form you can make is a loop of masking tape. If you make loop upon loop, you can create a facade, a piece of furniture or a room.

Soft pavilion

Did you know

... that Scotch tape was invented in 1930 by Richard Drew, a young American engineer? It soon became a very popular material for mending a wide variety of things. Duct tape was invented during World War II and was used to keep moisture out of the ammunition cases, but today it is used for everything. Even astronauts have used it when repairing a broken vehicle on the Moon.

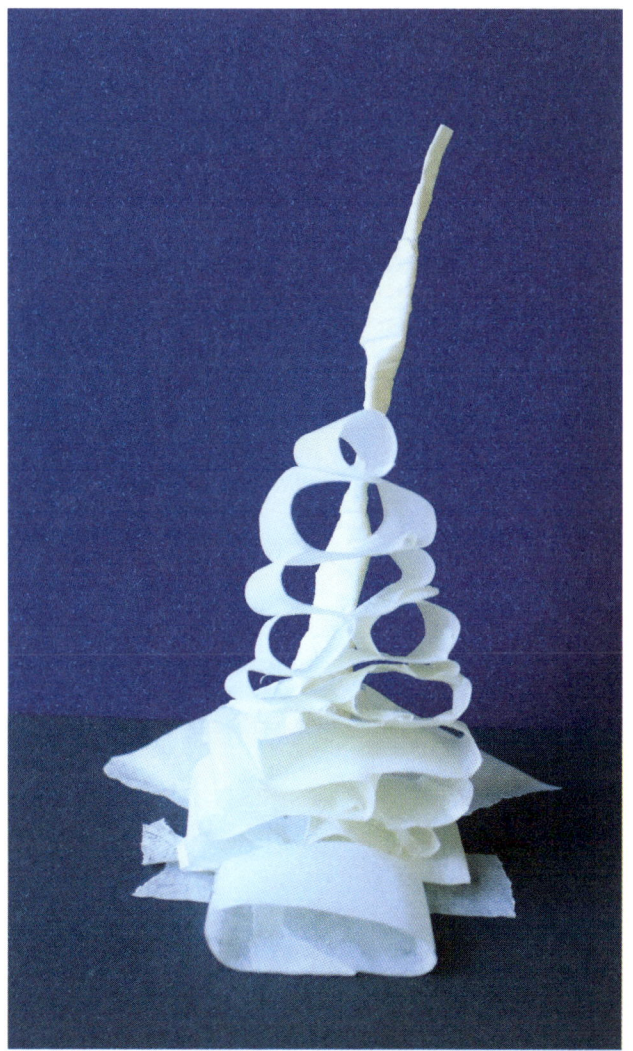

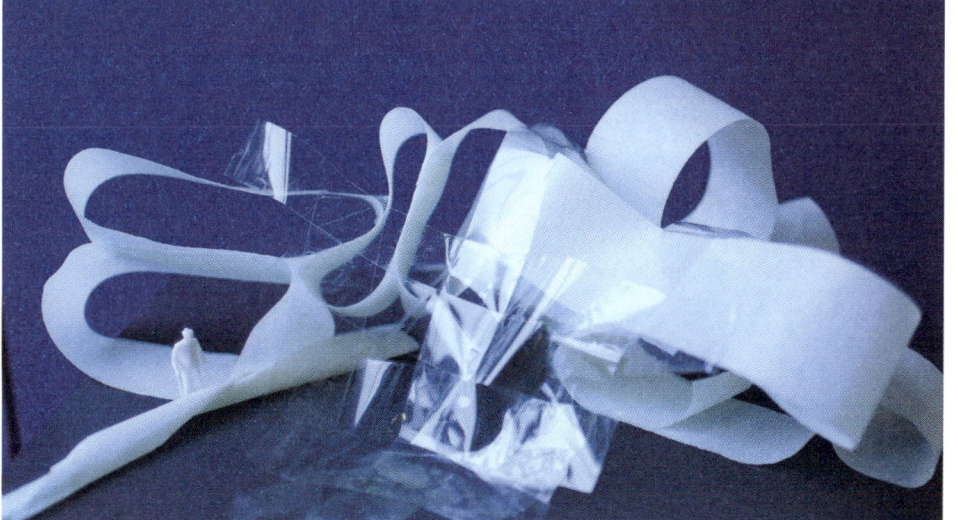

You can use all kinds of tape – masking tape, duct tape, coloured tape or patterned tape. Remember to insert a scale figure so that the scale of your pavilion is clear.

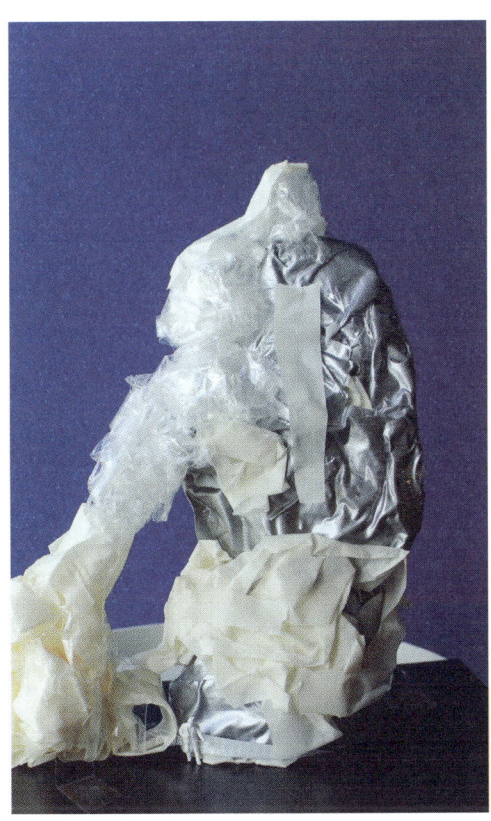

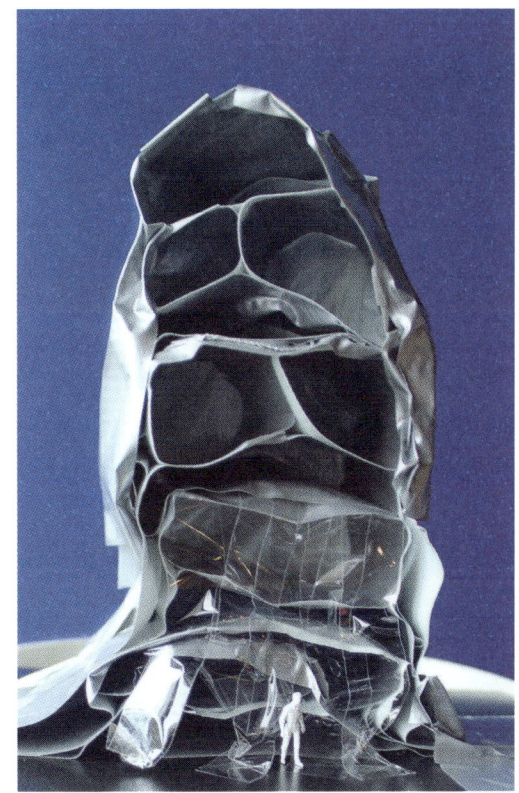

Serpentine Sackler Gallery

A light and elegant construction

Every summer a well-known architect is invited to design a temporary pavilion for Kensington Gardens in London. This tradition began in 2000 with a geometric pavilion by the architect Zaha Hadid. In 2007 Hadid was asked to design another temporary structure for the park. This pavilion comprised soft fabric structures resembling flowers giving shelter to people in the park.

Apart from the temporary pavilions, Kensington Gardens now contains a permanent pavilion by Zaha Hadid. The pavilion is part of the Serpentine Sackler Gallery, and it functions as an extension to an old historic building, which used to be a gunpowder store. This building now contains the gallery's exhibition space.

The gallery extension is an elegant, white structure and provides contrast to the heavy old building. The extension looks as if it could almost take off if it had not been anchored to the existing building.

Architect

Zaha Hadid
Iraq/Great Britain, b. 1950

Project

Serpentine Sackler Gallery
London, Great Britain, 2013

Soft form

The pavilion uses an advanced digital and geometric language and incorporates patterns and shapes only made possible by computer modelling. However, many of these forms are found to occur in nature. The fibreglass construction of the pavilion does look like a butterfly or a piece of bone – or a piece of fabric falling softly to the ground. The interior of the pavilion has the same organic design language of soft lines and large light surfaces. The structure of the pavilion has built-in lighting, so at night the pavilion appears lit up between the dark trees in the park.

Soft pavilion

Zaha Hadid

The Iraqi-British architect Zaha Hadid is the first female architect to be awarded the Pritzker Architecture Prize. Hadid is known for experimenting with form, and her interest in architecture started at an early age, when she designed the interior for her own bedroom.

Before studying architecture in London, she studied mathematics at the American University in Beirut.

Hadid was one of the first architects to use computer in the design of her buildings. The conditions of a project – such as climate, wind conditions and the number of future occupants working and living in the building – are fed into special computer software. With complex mathematical programmes the computer converts the information into a building form, which the architect can then work on. This technique is called parametric design. In Hadid's designs the result is often floating and futuristic architecture, forms which are visible in all her work, from buildings and furniture to shoes, jewellery and yachts.

The pavilion is light and airy with notable white columns and a built-in bar for the gallery guests.

Towering construction

Iron skeletons and load-bearing constructions are not just functional — they can also be beautiful and elegant. The French engineer Alexandre Gustav Eiffel was a master of these constructions. The Eiffel Tower — the highest tower in Paris — is a very good example of this. Construct a tower with a visible structure and experiment with materials, height and balance.

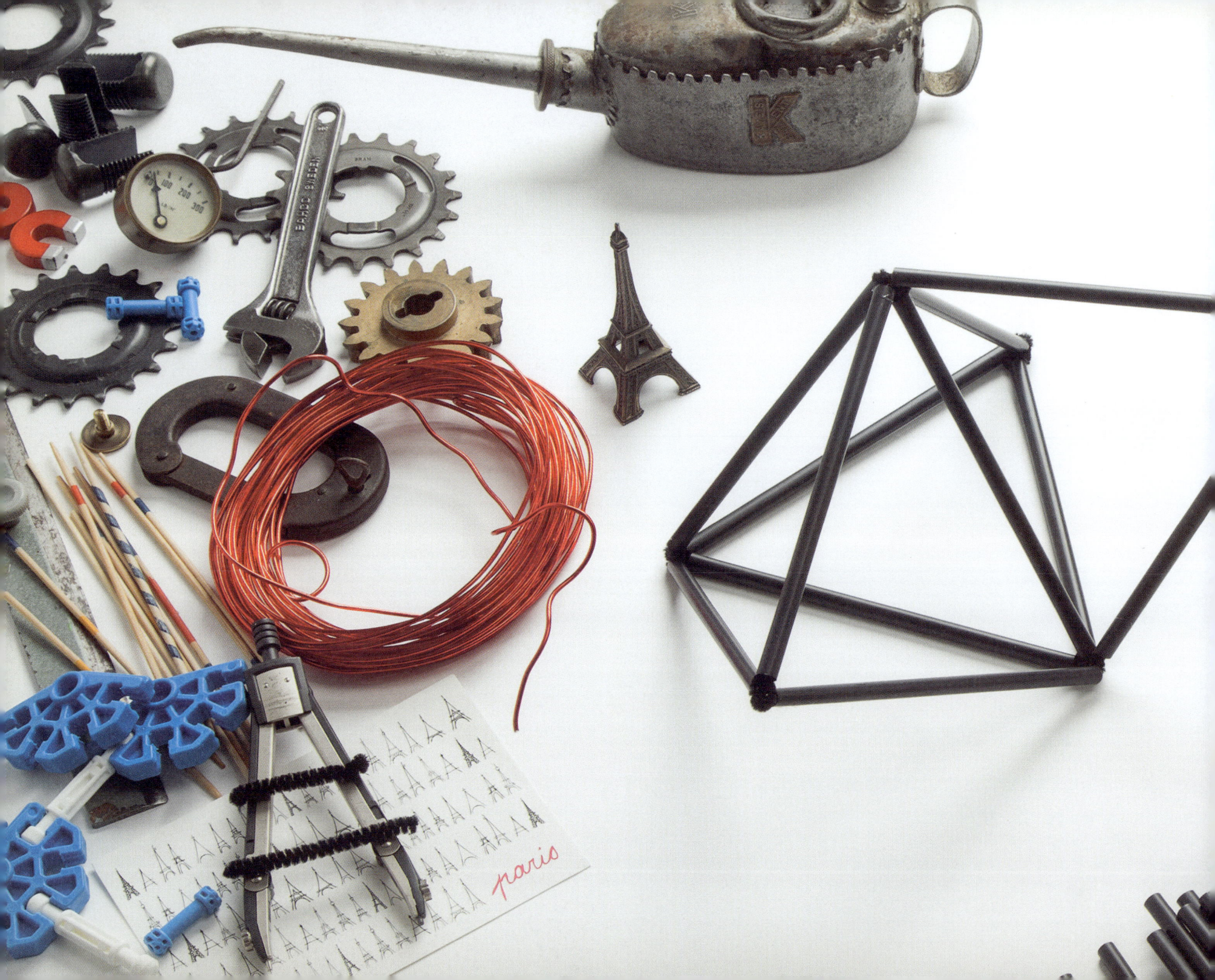

Towering constructions

Exercise

How many different towers do you know? Towers can be round, square, pointed or leaning. What they have in common is their height – especially compared with their surroundings.

Towers can have different functions, right from a lifeguard tower and a church tower to a water tower and an observation tower. Some towers are solid; others have an open, visible construction.

You can build your own open tower construction using black drinking straws and pipe cleaners. And why not add scale to your tower using scale figures and footbridges.

 Materials

- Black drinking straws
- White or black pipe cleaners
- Cardboard

 Tools

- Scissors
- Glue gun
- Possibly a scale figure in an appropriate size

Did you know

... that 2.5 million rivets were used in the Eiffel Tower construction?
... that 1,665 steps take you to the top?
... that 40 tons of paint is used to paint the tower every seventh
   year?

What to do

1   *Start by cutting off the "bend" (the short piece) of a handful of straws. Then cut some pipe cleaners into ca three-centimetre long pieces.*

2   *Build a two-dimensional (flat) triangle using three straws and three pipe cleaner connectors. Use your gluegun to fasten the joints.*

3   *You now have a two-dimensional triangle. Make sure to leave a bit of space between the straws, making room for more connectors as the construction grows.*

4   *Make the triangle three-dimensional by adding three more straws and connectors.*

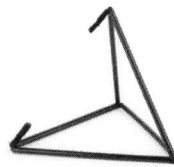

5   *If there is no room in the straw for more connectors, you can wrap them around an existing joint.*

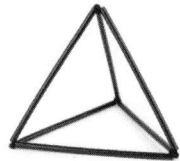

6   *You now have a pyramid construction consisting of four triangles.*

7   *Put more pyramids together, creating a base for your tower construction.*

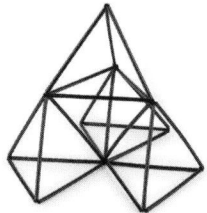

8   *Add one more triangle, giving your construction some height.*

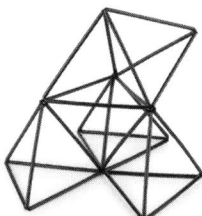

9   *Now you know the construction principle, and you can continue like this forever – give it a try.*

Tip

You decide whether your tower is going to be triangular, square or another geometrical shape. The triangle is the best shape if you want a strong and stable construction. If you want to build a square instead, you can make it stable by dividing it up into two triangles with an extra diagonal.

You can cut out some cardboard floors or footbridges and glue them onto your tower construction together with some scale figures. In this way you can add scale to your construction.

The smaller the figures, the higher the construction. In this way you can change the size of your building without changing the construction. (Read more about scale in the chapter on *Scale*).

You can also build a suspended, triangular tent construction. The two sides of the triangle are composed of fabric. The floor can be made of timber battens or heavy cardboard. Remember some string, so that the construction can be suspended.

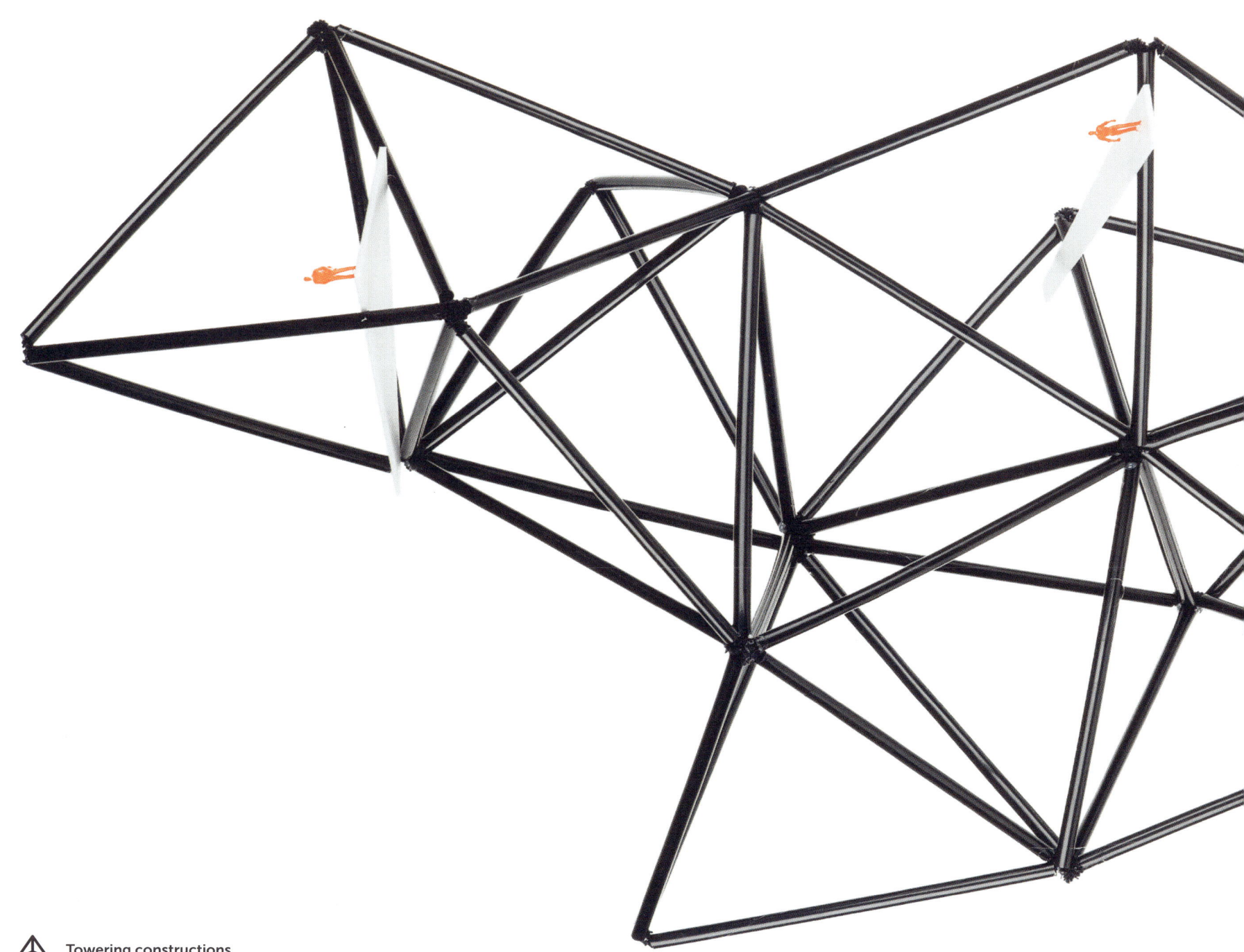

Towering constructions

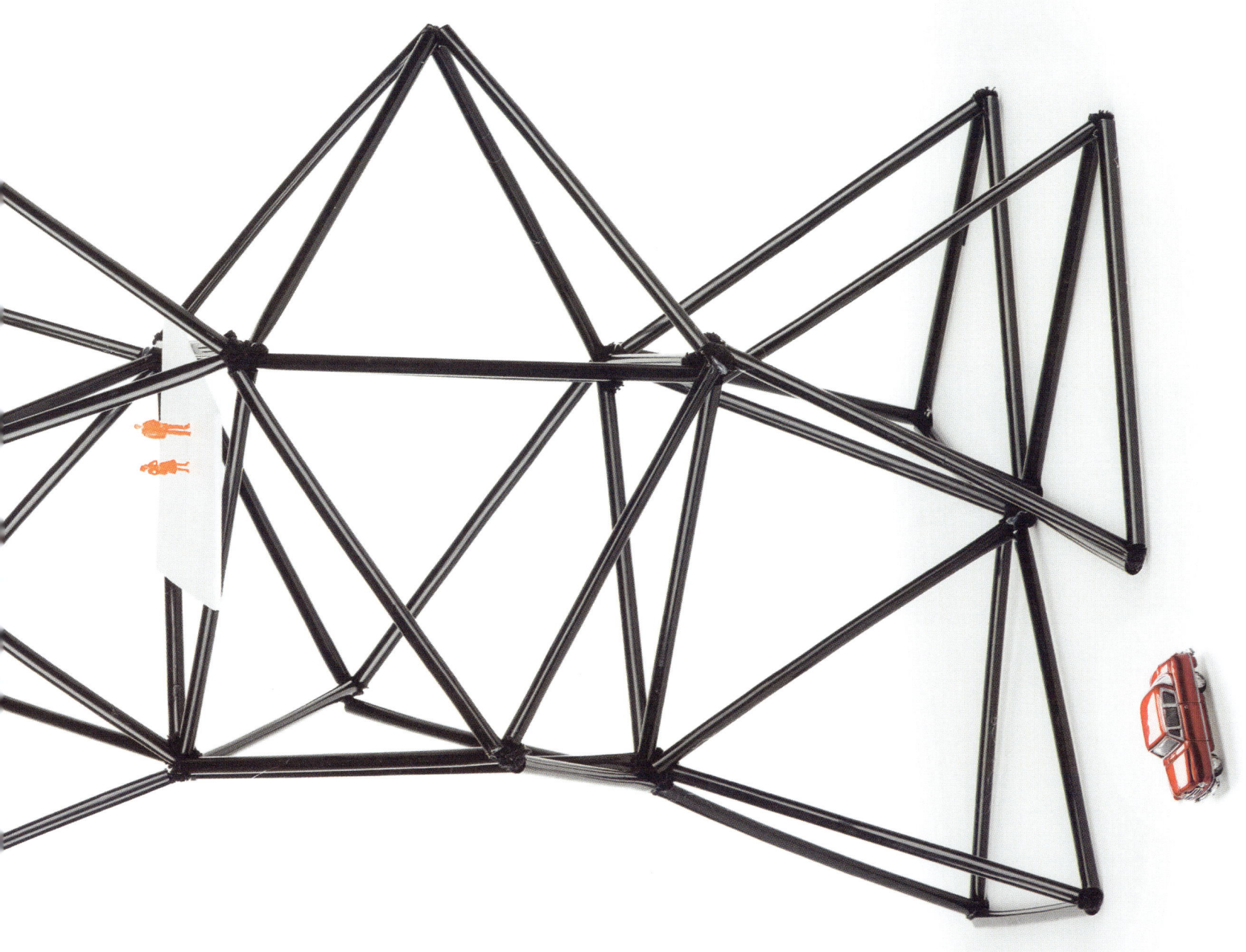

The Eiffel Tower

A naked iron skeleton

The Eiffel Tower is one of the most famous architectural icons in the world. But it has not always been so. When the tower was constructed in 1889 for the Paris World Exposition, it was met with opposition. People had never seen anything like it in the city – a 300-meter high naked iron skeleton. The tower, the world's highest at the time, looked gigantic and dominating next to its surroundings.

Originally, the idea was that the tower should be a temporary building, which could be taken down after 20 years. But as the height of the tower proved to be perfect for radio aerials, it was allowed a permanent status. Today the Eiffel Tower has become a symbol of France and Paris, and nobody is talking about taking it down any more. On the contrary, it has become a popular spot for outings. The tower is considered one of the most beautiful buildings in the world.

 Architect

Alexandre Gustave Eiffel
France, 1832-1923

 Bygningsværk

Eiffel Tower
Paris, France, 1889

No matter where you are in Paris, you can catch sight of the 300-meter high, iconic Eiffel Tower.

New times — new possibilities

In the 18th century the Industrial Revolution arrived, bringing with it great changes to society. Many innovations were made, changing everyday life as well as how the world was understood. The steam engine, the automobile, the bicycle, the telephone, the record player, the camera, the motion picture camera and many more new inventions became commonplace.

The Industrial Age also meant completely new building materials such as cast iron. Now it was possible to build constructions which were lighter, larger and taller than the traditional stone and brick architecture. And it was possible to shape the new material in many ways.

The Eiffel Tower is a cast iron, skeleton structure — in architectural terms, an "honest" construction, because everything is visible. This means minimum weight regarding materials and maximum strength regarding bearing capacity. The open structure makes the tower seem light despite its height. At the same time, it is difficult to say what is inside and what is outside. Are you inside the tower when you are enjoying the view from high up? In a way the Eiffel Tower became a symbol of the Industrial Revolution and an omen that times were changing. The possibility of a bird's eye view provided a new understanding of the city and the landscape around the tower.

The tower is grounded on its four legs, standing in the long Champ de Mars Park next to the Seine. The legs of the tower contain lifts and staircases, making it possible to get really close to the structure.

Even today the Eiffel Tower can be seen from far away – also at night when it is beautifully and dramatically lit. The function of the tower, the viewing platforms, can be spotted from far away, as the three floors are clearly visible. Apart from the viewing platforms, the tower also has two restaurants, an indoor exhibition space and a champagne bar at the top. At the very top there is a mast with radio and TV aerials as well as a weather station. And in the winter you can go ice skating at a temporary ice rink in the tower.

Alexandre Gustave Eiffel

The engineer Alexandre Gustave Eiffel was the brain behind the design as well as the engineering calculations. Before the tower he was better known for his bridge constructions in cast iron. Originally he trained as an engineer and therefore had special knowledge about iron. This knowhow took him around the world to countries like Vietnam, Brazil, Mexico, Angola, Peru, Bolivia and Chile, where you can find hundreds of constructions designed by Eiffel; and for New York he designed the internal construction of the Statue of Liberty. His bridge design for rail transportation gave him, and many other people, the chance to travel abroad.

Despite all his projects around the world, the Eiffel Tower is the most important and best-known building of Eiffel's career. Special calculations and dimensioning on the 300-meter high tower had to be done so it could resist the strong winds. In those days they did not have our advanced computer programmes to do the calculations. And therefore it was a great engineering accomplishment to do both the calculations on the construction principles and on the wind conditions for the tallest building in the world.

Building with prefab

Sometimes building something unique out of prefabricated standard elements can be a challenge. However, the American architect couple Ray and Charles Eames' own house is a very fine example of how it is possible to turn prefabricated materials into something very special. Build a composition out of prefabricated materials and turn it into an architectural work of art.

Building with prefab

Exercise

Architectural models can be made in many different ways and with all kinds of materials. One way,
for example, is to use a lot of the same material in
the same colour, such as corks, milk bottle tops or
LEGO® bricks. They are called prefabricated materials,
because they were made as part of a big production
for a specific use, other than model making.

Try creating an architectural composition comprising
only of prefabricated materials. Use only a few types
of material, but many repetitions of them. When you
have finished your composition take a photo of it,
colour it in and turn it into an architectural work of art.

Materials

- Drawing paper
- Heavy photocopying paper
- Prefabricated building materials like:
  KAPLA or LEGO® bricks (or other kinds of blocks)
- Tin cans (without the labels)
- Corks
- Cardboard tubes
- Possibly ludo or domino pieces

Tools

- Camera
- Printer
- Oil pastels, crayons, watercolours or felt-tip pens
- Possibly a scale figure in an appropriate size
- Possibly a photocopier

What to do

1. Build a composition using a maximum of three different prefabricated materials.
   - Use at least 10 KAPLA or LEGO® bricks.
   - Mark the entrance to your building.
   - Your composition must contain a minimum of one room.

2. Take a photo of your composition. Before taking your photo, remember to use a "calm" background, for example a white wall or a piece of plain coloured cardboard.

3. Print the photo in black and white on some heavy paper. If possible, give your print a lighter tone in the photocopier. You can choose the full motif or you can zoom in on a detail or an interesting space in your photo.

4. Select the objects in your photo that you want to colour in. It is a good idea to leave some elements in black and white. Leave the wooden blocks without colour so that their grain is visible, making a clear distinction between materials. By doing this, your choice of materials is visible in the composition.

5. Use oil pastels, crayons, watercolours or felt-tip pens. Choose the colours you want to use. You can create a nice graphic expression by selecting just a few different colours.

Eames House

A box on a hill

Steel, glass and coloured panels. That is all the Eames House comprises. It may sound simple and that is precisely what makes the house so special. All the materials are prefabricated standard elements. This means that no materials were made especially for the house. On the contrary, the materials are standard sizes and can be bought in a typical builders' merchant or DIY shop.

The Eames House is situated in Pacific Palisades near Los Angeles. It was designed by the American architect couple Ray and Charles Eames. For nearly 30 years the house functioned as both their home and studio, where they lived and worked together. The house is known especially for the architects' creative use of standard elements, the pattern of colourful squares on the facade and for blending in with its surroundings.

 Architect

Ray Eames
USA, 1912-1988

Charles Eames
USA, 1907-1978

 Project

Eames House
Los Angeles, USA, 1949

The Eames House is constructed of steel, glass and coloured panels. None of the building materials were made especially for the house – they are all prefabricated standard elements.

A modern house

Ray and Charles Eames got the idea for the Eames House at the end of the 1940s when they were asked to design a modern home. After World War ll there was a great need for more housing in the USA, in particular for soldiers returning home from the war.

The American magazine Arts and Architecture therefore invited different architects to develop proposals for a modern house. It was called the Case Study House Programme and it was meant as an inspiration and demonstration of how to build good, inexpensive housing that was easy to construct. To use prefabricated standard elements was therefore an obvious solution. Apart from the rule that the houses had to be functional, they also had to live up to the needs or demands of the users. Ray and Charles Eames were asked to design and build a house for a couple which would suit their own needs.

The Eames House, a two-storey rectangular box, is situated on a hill overlooking the Pacific Ocean. The load-bearing structure consists of black steel beams and columns. The gaps are filled with glass and coloured panels. In addition, large windows allow for daylight to flood the house. This kind of construction makes the house look very lightweight.

When you look at the floor plan, you can see that the house is split in two, with the living areas at one end and a studio at the other. In between there is an open courtyard. Having a living space and work space so close to each other was perfect for the Eames couple and their way of life.

There are 25 Case Study Houses in total in the USA. The Eames House is number eight in the series and it has become known as Case Study House No. 8. Today the house is owned by the Eames Foundation and it functions as a museum.

First floor

Living room

Bedroom

Studio

Ground floor

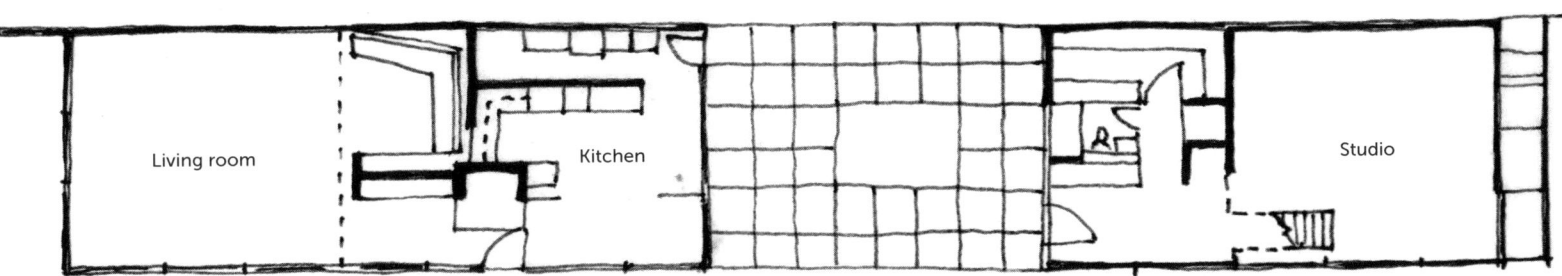

Living room

Kitchen

Studio

Floor plan of the Eames House, showing how the couple's home (to the left) is separated from the studio by a courtyard.

Ray og Charles Eames

Ray and Charles Eames are among just a few architects who have formed a partnership both privately and professionally. In fact, they were not qualified architects. Charles Eames did study architecture at Washington University, but he never finished his degree. Instead he opened up his own practice and began teaching at the Cranbrook Academy of Art in Michigan. He met Ray, an artist, at the academy and they married in 1941. In the same year they moved to Los Angeles and started their own practice together.

Ray and Charles Eames are world-renowned for more than their house. They have made art and created graphics, designed exhibitions, toys, films and furniture. In fact, their furniture has been a huge success with several of the chairs still being produced today, such as the Lounge Chair Metal (LCM).

Did you know

... that Charles Eames was fond of clowns and that he made a film of how to paint oneself as a clown? The film is called "Clown Face" and for many years it was shown to new students at the Clown College, teaching them how to apply clown makeup.

Glossary

Aesthetics
The branch of philosophy concerned with the study of concepts relating to the senses - not just about beauty.

Additive
Characterized by, relating to, or produced by addition.

ARC
The Amager Resource Centre: a Danish energy plant converting waste products to energy.

Art Nouveau
A decorative style of art, architecture and design employing curved, graceful lines, prevalent in Western Europe and the USA from about 1890 until 1914.

Beam (structure)
A horizontal structural element, supported at each end by walls, columns or piers.

Bird's eye view
Perspective, as seen from a bird's eye while flying on high.

Building regulations
Set of rules to be followed.

Calliper
A device used to measure the distance between two opposite sides of an object.

Carte blanche
A blank card, in French; used to mean a free hand.

Cast iron
A moulded iron alloy, allowing e.g. structures to be built high due to its load-bearing capacity.

Column (structure)
A vertical structural element, used as support or decoration or both.

Commission
To employ for a specific purpose or that purpose itself; example: to commission an architect to design a house.

Component
A part of something more complex.

Composition
Arrangement of artistic parts so as to form a unified whole.

Comprising
To consist of.

Contrast
Strikingly different to something else.

Crypt
A stone chamber beneath the floor of a church, usually used for burial.

Design language
*All-encompassing scheme that defines
the work of a specific form or style.*

Dimension
A measurable extent, such as length, width, breadth, depth.

Dome
A rounded vault forming the roof of a structure.

Elevation
The facade of a building or its accurate reproduction.

Facade
The face of a building.

Facility
Something created to serve a particular function.

Fibreglass
*A strong material made of fine glass fibres bonded with synthetic
resin, used in the construction of cars, boats etc.*

Functionalism 1920-1940
*The belief that the design of objects should be determined
by their function rather than by aesthetic considerations.*

Geometry
*In mathematics dealing with relationships between
points, lines, surfaces and solids.*

Graphics
Any of the fine or applied visual arts based on drawing.

High-tech
*High technology; using, involving or requiring the latest
technological solutions, materials or processes.*

Horizontal ribbon windows
*Windows, longer than high, that resemble the shape
of a ribbon; this kind of window is enabled by the use
of reinforced columns instead of load-bearing walls.*

Icon
*Regarded as a representative symbol or
worthy of great respect.*

Incorporating
To take in or contain something as part of a whole.

Industrial design
*Refers to products that are developed by applied art and
applied science to improve the aesthetics, ergonomics,
functionality and usability of a product and its production.*

Industrial Revolution
*The transformation of society from agricultural
to industrial in the 18th-19th centuries.*

Load-bearing (structure)
*Refers to weight distribution and support in building
constructions. For example, walls are load-bearing.*

Module
A standardized and independent unit that can be used to construct a more complex structure.

Ocean liner
A large luxurious passenger ship of the type once used on a regular line or route.

Organic
Based on nature's harmonious forms and order.

Parametric
A set of measurable factors, such as temperature and number of users, that define a system.

Paris World Exposition
The last great national exposition, held in Paris in 1844, which gave way to regular World Expos.

Patron
A person who gives financial or other support to another person, organisation or cause.

Perspective
The art of representing a three-dimensional object on a two-dimensional surface, giving the right impression of size.

Polemicist
A person who argues in opposition to others.

Polystyrene
A synthetic resin which is a polymer of styrene, used chiefly as lightweight stiff foam or film.

Practice (architectural)
A firm or company that employs one or more architects and performs the practices of professional architecture.

Prefabricated
Manufactured sections (of building or furniture) for speedy assembly.

Pritzker Architecture Prize
One of the most prestigious prizes in the world, awarded annually to a living architect.

RIBA
The Royal Institute of British Architects; its most prestigious award is the Gold Medal.

Scale
The relative size or extent of something; a range of values forming a standard system of measurement.

Standard (element, size)
Agreed norms of dimensions for specific objects.

Structure
A way of building; arranging parts in a certain way for the purpose of holding them together in a stable relationship.

Survey
*A serious examination of something in order
to ascertain its qualities and potential.*

Transform
Make a marked change in form, nature or appearance.

Urban space
An open space within a town or city.

Worm's eye view
*Perspective, seen from the view of a worm
crawling on the ground.*

The authors and the publisher wish to thank
the following for their kind contribution of photos:

Jens Hemmel (all photos apart from the ones listed below)

Flemming Bo Andersen (page 45)
Iwan Baan/Herzog & de Meuron (page 57 – photo no. 3)
Henriette Bendix (pages 131, 133)
BIG – Bjarke Ingels Group (pages 61, 62, 63)
Bo Bolther (pages 89, 117, 118, 119)
Julie Dufour (pages 46, 47, 69, 71, 87,144, 145, 161, 163)
Eames Office© 2014 LLC (pages 175, 176)
Gehl Architects/DOT (pages 73, 74, 75)
Luke Hayes (pages 147, 149)
Jannes Linders/Benthem Crouwel Architects (page 57 – photo no. 2)
Rebecca Lomholt (pages 103, 105)
Thomas Mølvig (page 48)
Nick Weall (page 57 – photo no. 1)

About the authors

Malene Abildgaard, b. 1979
Architect MAA
The Aarhus School of
Architecture, Denmark.

Julie Dufour, b. 1967
Architect MAA
The Royal Danish Academy of Fine
Arts, School of Architecture, Denmark.

Malene has worked for several years with the dissemination of architecture for children and young people at the Utzon Centre and the Danish Architecture Centre, among other places. She is the architect behind "Attend architecture in your spare time", an extracurricular course for children and young people with an interest in the subject.

See her website at www.maleneabildgaard.dk

Julie has wide experience working with the dissemination of architecture through workshops in Denmark and abroad. She teaches children and young people at the Danish Architecture Centre, the Children's Culture House Ama'r and Farum School of Art. In addition, she runs family workshops aimed at parents and children at numerous cultural institutions in Denmark.

See her website at www.juliedufour.dk.

For more information about the authors' joint projects, see www.mylittlearchitect.com

Build, draw & learn with world-famous architects

Text © Malene Abildgaard, Julie Dufour and ABC Forlag, 2014

Photo: Jens Hemmel
Art direction, cover and graphical principles: Fie Sahl Kreutzfeldt
Publishing and editing: Flemming Møldrup
The publication is set in Museo Sans
Printed in Slovenia
1st edition, 1st printing

ISBN 978-87-7916-285-3
www.abc-forlag.dk